Table of Contents

 ISBN 0-88724-498-X

About the Book

Grammar Grades 3-4

Prepared By: Kelley Wingate Levy
Written By: Susan Taylor Drumm

This book is just one in our Best Value™ series of reproducible, skill-oriented activity books. Each book is developmentally appropriate and contains over 100 pages packed with educationally-sound, classroom-tested activities. Each book also contains skill cards and resource pages with extended activity ideas.

The activities in this book have been developed to help students master the basic skills necessary to succeed in grammar. The activities have been sequenced to help insure successful completion of the assigned tasks, thus building positive self-esteem, as well as the self-confidence students need to meet academic challenges.

The activities may be used by themselves, as supplemental activities, or as enrichment material for a grammar program.

Developed by teachers and tested by students, we never lost sight of the fact that if students don't stay motivated and involved, they will never truly grasp the skills being taught on a cognitive level.

About the Author...

Susan Taylor Drumm has been a teacher for over ten years. Susan taught primarily middle grades. She instructed an Academic Resource Lab that focused on students in need of organizational and study skills. Susan has also worked at a cooperative preschool and has home schooled her three children: Eli, Abigail, and Hannah. She holds a B.S. in secondary education, an M.Ed. in reading, and is a certified reading specialist.

Ready-to-Use Ideas and Activities

The activities in this book will help children master the basic skills necessary to become competent learners. Remember as you read through the activities listed below and as you go through this book, that all children learn at their own rates. Although repetition is important, it is critical that we never lose sight of the fact that it is equally important to build children's self-esteem and self-confidence if we want them to become successful learners.

Flashcard Ideas

The back of this book has removable skill cards that will be helpful for basic skill and enrichment activities. Pull the skill cards out and cut them apart (if you have access to a paper cutter, use that). Following are several ideas for use of the skill cards.

- Reproduce the skill-card sheet on the next page in this book, making enough to have one for each student. Hand them out to the students. Take the skill cards and write the words on the chalk board. Have the students choose 24 of the words and write them in any order on the empty spaces of their skill card sheets, writing only one word in each space. When all students have finished their cards, make the skill cards into a deck. Call out the words one at a time. Any student who has a word that is called out should make an "X" through the word to cross it out. The first student who crosses out five words in a row (horizontally, vertically, or diagonally) wins the game. To extend the game you can continue playing until a student crosses out all the words on his bingo sheet.

- Give each student three or four cards. Call out a part of speech (noun, verb, adjective) and have students hold up words that belong to that category.

- Have students categorize the words into designated groups. Use the categorized groups to create "silly sentences."

- Have students alphabetize the cards as they read the words aloud.

- Use specific card words as a guide for studying a particular assignment.

Skill Card Sheet

		FREE		

Name ______________________________ **Noun Recognition**

A **noun** is a word that names a person, place, or thing.

Examples:	**person**	Frosty the Snowman
	place	North Pole
	thing	snowflake

Circle the words below that are nouns.

igloo	coldly	fished	Eskimo
Alaska	seal	icy	sled
son	skated	otter	frozen
snow	freezing	canoe	polar bear
storm	followed	frost	dogs

Circle the nouns in each sentence. The number tells you how many there are.

1. The Eskimo paddled his kayak through the icy water. (3)
2. His son sat excitedly in the boat. (2)
3. They were going to town to pick up a gift. (2)
4. The gift was a puppy. (2)
5. The puppy would be the new dog to pull their sled. (3)
6. The puppy would also be their friend. (2)
7. The Eskimo and his son arrived at the pet store. (3)
8. They hugged the puppy. (1)

Name ______________________________

Noun Recognition

A **noun** is a word that names a person, place, or thing.

Example: Ranger Rick park moose

Read the nouns below and write them in the correct columns.

Dr. Doolittle	**Adams Park**	**tree**
shoe	**New York**	**Mr. Ranger**
Mr. Canyon	**Karen's Café**	**Buffalo Bill**
wildflower	**box**	**Western Inn**
picnic	**Harry**	**Ohio**

Person	Place	Thing
______________	______________	______________
______________	______________	______________
______________	______________	______________
______________	______________	______________
______________	______________	______________

Circle the nouns in each sentence. The number tells you how many there are.

1. **My family visited Yellowstone National Park. (2)**
2. **Yellowstone has amazing sites. (2)**
3. **We saw moose, elk, and buffalo. (3)**
4. **There are geysers, where hot water and steam shoot out of the ground. (4)**

Name ____________________________________

A **common noun** names any person, place, or thing.

Examples:	Common Nouns	Not Common Nouns
	store	Joe's Market
	uncle	Uncle Bruce
	dog	Snoopy

Circle the common noun in each pair of words below.

1. cow	Bessie	6. book	*Ted the Toad*
2. park	Lincoln Park	7. Christmas	holiday
3. Rouge River	river	8. May	month
4. doctor	Doctor Baker	9. girl	Sarah
5. Chicago	city	10. day	Monday

Circle the common noun in each sentence.

1. My cat is named Frisky.
2. Julie is my cousin.
3. My favorite drink is Kool Kola.
4. We eat turkey on Thanksgiving Day.
5. On Monday I go to school.
6. Iceland is a country I want to visit.
7. My house is on Main Street.
8. Her name is Rose.
9. My favorite holiday is Valentine's Day.
10. Is your cat's name Fluffy?

Name ______________________________

A **common noun** names any person, place, or thing.

Examples:	Common Nouns	Not Common Nouns
	boat	Titanic
	ocean	Pacific Ocean
	sailor	Captain Cook

Circle the common nouns in each sentence. The number tells you how many there are.

1. **Boats are used all over the world. (2)**
2. **The first boats were developed from rafts. (2)**
3. **Ancient Egyptians were the first people to add sails to boats. (3)**
4. **Native Americans and early settlers used canoes. (2)**
5. **A canoe is a long, thin boat moved by paddles. (3)**
6. **A ship is a large boat made to travel on oceans. (3)**
7. **Ships carry passengers and freight, and are used to fight battles. (4)**
8. **Two famous ships are the Mayflower and the Santa Maria. (1)**

Read the clues and write the common noun they describe.

______________________ **1. I hold coffee and you drink from me.**

______________________ **2. You use me to call people. I have push buttons and you hold me to your ear.**

______________________ **3. I have a keyboard and a monitor. Many people use me when they write and work.**

______________________ **4. I am a furry pet that barks.**

Name ______________________________ **Proper Nouns**

A **proper noun** names a specific person, place, or thing.

Examples:	George Washington	Virginia
	White House	Rover

Days of the week, months of the year, holidays, and book titles are also proper nouns.

Examples:	Monday	Valentine's Day
	June	*United States History*

Read the nouns listed below. Write the proper nouns in the blanks.

Mount Vernon	**president**	**Martha Washington**
general	**February**	**Revolutionary War**
Presidents' Day	**state**	**colony**
horse	**leader**	**General Washington**
Mrs. Brown	**paper**	**December**

Proper Nouns

______________________ ______________________

______________________ ______________________

______________________ ______________________

______________________ ______________________

Circle the proper nouns in each sentence.

1. **George Washington lived in the state of Virginia.**
2. **George Washington first proved himself a leader when he was a general.**
3. **He led the American Colonies to victory during the Revolutionary War.**
4. **He was then elected to be the first president of the United States.**
5. **He and his wife, Martha, lived in a home known as Mount Vernon.**

Name ______________________________ **Proper Nouns**

A **proper noun** names a specific person, place, or thing and is always capitalized.

Examples:	Harold Hill	Lake Michigan
	Krispy Krinkles	Lassie

Days of the week, months of the year, holidays, and book titles are also proper nouns.

Examples:	Tuesday	Mother's Day
	March	*Max and the Mud Pie Mystery*

Fill in each blank with a proper noun.

1. **A holiday I like is ______________________________.**
2. **One of my relatives is named ______________________________.**
3. **The last book I read was ______________________________.**
4. **One of the summer months is ______________________________.**
5. **The day of the week today is ______________________________.**
6. **The state where I was born is ______________________________.**
7. **The day of the week yesterday was ______________________________.**
8. **A restaurant I like is called ______________________________.**
9. **My favorite month is ______________________________.**
10. **My mother's name is ______________________________.**

Write the proper noun from each sentence in the blank.

______________________ **1. My dog's name is Inspector.**

______________________ **2. Mary had her cat, Candy, with her.**

______________________ **3. Last week I went to Canada.**

Name ________________________________

Common & Proper Noun Review

Common nouns name any one of a group of persons, places, or things.
Proper nouns name a specific person, place, or thing.

Write each noun below in the column where it belongs.

state	**Uncle Joe**	**President Truman**
Japan	**Tweety**	**planet**
forest	**Yosemite Park**	**cousin**
dollar	**orange**	**Mayflower**

Common Nouns	Proper Nouns
______________________	______________________
______________________	______________________
______________________	______________________
______________________	______________________
______________________	______________________
______________________	______________________

Read the paragraph below. Circle the common nouns (14) and underline the proper nouns (14).

A Famous Monument

The Black Hills of South Dakota are home to a towering and majestic monument. The monument, called Mount Rushmore, is a beautiful carving in the side of a mountain. The carving is of four great presidents: George Washington, Thomas Jefferson, Abraham Lincoln, and Teddy Roosevelt. Mount Rushmore was carved by a sculptor named Gutzon Borglum. Borglum and his crew spent four-teen years carving Mount Rushmore. Today it stands as a symbol of the United States. A trip to the state of South Dakota is not complete without a visit to Mount Rushmore.

Name ______________________________

Common & Proper Noun Review

Common nouns name any one of a group of persons, places, or things.
Proper nouns name a specific person, place, or thing.

Each sentence has one common noun and one proper noun. Write the common noun to the left of the sentence and the proper noun to the right.

Common Nouns		Proper Nouns
song	My favorite song is Edelweiss.	*Edelweiss*
________	Smokey is a famous bear.	________
________	My family ate at Pizza Barn.	________
________	Ogden is a beautiful city.	________
________	Isaac Newton was a scientist.	________
________	The first satellite was Sputnik I.	________
________	George Eastman made cameras.	________
________	The Pilgrims sailed for two months.	________
________	Emily Dickinson was a poet.	________

Write a common noun AND a proper noun for each category.

	Common	Proper
1. a place to visit	________	________
2. a place to play	________	________
3. a neighbor	________	________

Name ________________________________

Common & Proper Noun Review

Circle all proper nouns in the sentences below. Underline all the common nouns. (The first number after the sentence tells how many proper nouns are in the sentence. The second number tells how many common nouns there are.)

1. The Pony Express was the first direct-mail service to the western territories of North America. (2, 2)
2. The Pony Express started in St. Joseph, Missouri, and ended in Sacramento, California. (3, 0)
3. The Pony Express was started in January, 1860, by a company named Russell, Majors, and Waddell. (3, 1)
4. This service delivered mail from Missouri to California in ten days! (2, 3)
5. Riders passed through eight states, crossing rivers, plains, and the Rocky Mountains, as they rode to the west coast. (1, 5)
6. The first rider left Missouri on April 3, 1860. (2, 1)
7. He arrived in Sacramento in nine days and 23 hours. (1, 2)
8. The first mail included a letter from President Buchanan to the governor of California. (2, 3)
9. The most famous rider for the Pony Express was William F. Cody, also known as Buffalo Bill. (3, 1)
10. The Pony Express was helpful, but it only lasted 18 months. (1, 1)
11. The telegraph had been invented by Samuel Morse. (1, 1)
12. A telegraph line was built across North America. (1, 1)
13. Messages were sent to California more quickly and safely by this telegraph. (1, 2)
14. The telegraph put an end to the Pony Express. (1, 2)

Name ______________________________

A **plural noun** names more than one person, place, or thing. Most nouns are made plural by adding **-s**.

Examples: friend<u>s</u> island<u>s</u> hamburger<u>s</u>

To make nouns ending in -*x*, -*s*, -*ch*, and -*sh* plural, add **-es**.

Examples: fox<u>es</u> guess<u>es</u> bench<u>es</u> wish<u>es</u>

Write the plural for each noun.

hunch ______________________ **reflex** ______________________

kangaroo ______________________ **miss** ______________________

porch ______________________ **machine** ______________________

Write the correct plural noun to complete each sentence.

1. **One of my birthday** ______________________ **came true!**
   (wish)
2. **I wished for a trip to City Island with my** ______________________.
   (friend)
3. **We did many wonderful** ______________________ **on City Island.**
   (thing)
4. **We sat on** ______________________ **and ate ice cream.**
   (bench)
5. **We played three** ______________________ **of Water Golf.**
   (round)
6. **We bought** ______________________ **and flew them.**
   (kite)
7. **Then we ate our** ______________________ **by the river.**
   (lunch)
8. **I wish there were more** ______________________ **like this.**
   (day)

Name ______________________________ **Plural Nouns**

A **plural noun** names more than one person, place, or thing. Most nouns are made plural by adding **-s**.

Examples: bakers gardens grapes

To make nouns ending in *-x*, *-s*, *-ch*, and *-sh* plural, add **-es**.

Examples: taxes glasses churches bushes

Complete the story below by adding the correct plural nouns.

I like many ______________ (kind) of fruits, but my mom knows that my favorite is ______________ (peach). One of my favorite ______________ (food) in the world is a juicy, peach pie. Mom doesn't make ______________ (pie) very often, though. Yesterday, she ran ______________ (errand) and came back with something special for me. She gave me three ______________ (guess) to find out what it was. My first guess was some ______________ (sock). My second guess was ______________ (bunch) of grapes. My third guess was some ______________ (pencil). Then mom showed me two ______________ (box) of ______________ (peach). "My favorite," I yelled as I gave mom two ______________ (kiss). "Peach pie for dessert," mom said and smiled.

Name ______________________________

A **plural noun** names more than one person, place, or thing.

To form the plural of a noun that ends with a consonant then **y**, change the **-y** to **-i** and add **-es**.

Examples: I rode a pony at the fair. Jim rode two ponies.

If the noun ends in a vowel then **y**, just add **-s**.

Examples: Dad lost his car key. Dad lost all his keys.

Write the plural form of each noun.

city	______________	**toy**	______________
cry	______________	**story**	______________
baby	______________	**tray**	______________

Write the correct plural nouns to complete each sentence.

1. **There are two** ______________ (library) **in our town.**
2. **Two** ______________ (lady) **work in the library by my house.**
3. **There are also two** ______________ (bakery) **in town.**
4. **They sell tarts with** ______________ (cherry) **for** ______________ (penny).
5. **Our town's pet store has** ______________ (guppy), ______________ (puppy), **and** ______________ (monkey)!

Name ______________________________ **Plural Nouns**

A **plural noun** names more than one person, place, or thing.

To form the plural of a noun that ends with a consonant then **-y**, change the **-y** to **-i** and add **-es**.

Examples: I live in a city. I have lived in three different cities.

If the noun ends in a vowel then -y, just add **-s**.

Examples: Our house has a chimney. Our last house had two chimneys.

Complete the sentences by adding the correct plural nouns.

Aunt Nancy's home is surrounded by hills and ______________________.
(valley)

Wild ______________________ grow in the valleys. When our
(berry)

______________________ got together this year, Aunt Nancy took all the
(family)

children berry picking. All my cousins, both the ______________________
(boy)

and the girls, loved picking ______________________. They tasted so
(berry)

good! We even found fruit trees with wild ______________________. A
(cherry)

large family of white ______________________ was playing in some
(bunny)

______________________. I hope we can stay with Aunt Nancy for many
(lily)

______________________ next year and pick ______________________
(day) (berry)

in the ______________________ again.
(valley)

Name ______________________________

A **plural noun** names more than one person, place, or thing. The plural of some nouns is formed with a brand new word. A few words are spelled the same whether they mean one or more than one.

Examples: Ted lost a tooth. Tracy lost two teeth.
Bambi is a deer. All the deer liked salt.

Match each noun on the left with its plural form on the right.

_______ **woman**	**A. feet**
_______ **sheep**	**B. children**
_______ **child**	**C. oxen**
_______ **moose**	**D. sheep**
_______ **foot**	**E. women**
_______ **ox**	**F. moose**

Complete each sentence with the plural form of the given noun. Use a dictionary if you are not sure.

1. **The trumpet players in the band were all ______________________.**
(man)
2. **My sister likes to feed the ______________________ at the park.**
(goose)
3. **We saw three white ______________________ and one black sheep.**
(sheep)
4. **My family has two grown-ups and two ______________________.**
(child)
5. **Tabby, our cat, caught five ______________________ last night.**
(mouse)

Name ______________________________ **Plural Noun Review**

Write the plural form of each noun.

fox ____________	**kite** ____________	**boy** ____________
city ____________	**tooth** ____________	**reflex** ____________
deer ____________	**child** ____________	**party** ____________
box ____________	**brush** ____________	**bus** ____________
valley ____________	**church** ____________	**paint** ____________

Write the plural form of the missing nouns to complete the paragraph. Use a dictionary if you are not sure.

Life for ______________ (cowboy) is exciting, but it is also hard work. Most cowboys work on big ______________ (ranch), taking care of all the ______________ (horse) and ______________ (cow). It is the cowboy's job to feed the ______________ (animal) and to make sure they stay healthy. Each year when ______________ (calf) are born, the cow-boys brand them and give them ______________ (shot). If a calf gets sick, then he gives the calf medicine ______________ (drop). Cowboys also put new ______________ (shoe) on horses and check their ______________ (tooth) to learn how old they are. They even mend ______________ (fence).

Name ________________________________ **Compound Nouns**

Nouns that are made up of two smaller nouns are called **compound nouns**.

Examples:	lighthouse	classroom	newspaper
	fireplace	cookbook	chalkboard

Match the words on the left with the words on the right to make compound nouns. Then write the words on the lines.

play	**crow**	**1.** ______________________
meat	**toes**	**2.** ______________________
sun	**boat**	**3.** ______________________
scare	**mate**	**4.** ______________________
sail	**set**	**5.** ______________________
tip	**loaf**	**6.** ______________________

Write the compound noun that completes each sentence.

1. **A fish shaped like a star is a** ______________________.
2. **An ache in your head is a** ______________________.
3. **A room for a bed is a** ______________________.
4. **The shore along the sea is the** ______________________.
5. **Light given by candles is** ______________________.
6. **A man who delivers mail is a** ______________________.
7. **A person who fights fires is a** ______________________.

Possessive Nouns

Story Hour

____

ho or what is the owner of something. To make a singular
strophe before the **s**.

all went through the hoop.

ssive, add an apostrophe after the **s**.

balls just hit the rim.

sentence so that it shows possession.
some are plural.)

______________________ **coach is Mr. Dribble.**
(team)

______________ **first name is Dan.**

______________ **favorite night is Friday.**
(Dan)

4. **Every Friday the** ______________________________ **gym is full of fans.**
(school)

5. ______________________________ **cheers can be heard in the stands.**
(Parents)

6. ______________________________ **pompons wave in the air.**
(Cheerleaders)

7. **The** ______________________________ **families cheer as the team wins.**
(players)

8. **The** ______________________________ **mascot does a cartwheel.**
(team)

9. **The** ______________________________ **bus takes everyone to the ice**
(school)
cream shop.

10. **The** ______________________________ **driver is named Mr. Ed.**
(bus)

Name ______________________________

A **possessive noun** shows who or what is the owner of something. To make a singular noun possessive add an apostrophe before the **s**.

Example: The jewelry <u>box's</u> diamonds were gone!

To make a plural noun possessive, add an apostrophe after the **s**.

Example: Police <u>cars'</u> sirens were heard everywhere.

Write each noun in the sentence so that it shows possession. Underline the thing that belongs or is owned by the noun. The first one has been done for you.

1. **The** ___*judge's*___ **<u>gavel</u> hit the bench and the trial began.**
   (judge)
2. **The** ______________ **noise stopped.**
   (courtroom)
3. **One lawyer told the jury what happened to** ______________ **diamonds.**
   (Mrs. Ruby)
4. **The** ______________ **speech went on for many hours.**
   (lawyer)
5. **By the end of the day, the** ______________ **whereabouts was still unclear.**
   (jewelry)
6. **Finally the** ______________ **voice was heard.**
   (judge)
7. **"Does your speech have anything to do with the** ______________ **disappearance?" he asked.**
   (diamonds)
8. **"You are testing the** ______________ **patience!"**
   (court)
9. **Suddenly a** ______________ **footsteps were heard.**
   (police officer)
10. **"I found the missing jewels in** ______________ **trunk!" he announced.**
    (Mrs. Ruby)

Name ______________________________ **Subject Pronouns**

A **pronoun** is a word that can take the place of a noun. *I, you, he, she, it, we*, and *they* are **subject pronouns**.

Examples: **Abraham Lincoln** was the 16th president.
He was the 16th president.

Betty loves art class
She loves art class

Change each sentence by using a pronoun in place of the underlined words.

1. **My friends are coming over today.**

   ______________________________ **are coming over today.**

2. **Frank and I love to go to the movies.**

   ______________________________ **love to go to the movies.**

3. **Maria is the best speller in our class.**

   ______________________________ **is the best speller in our class.**

4. **Jonathon reads a new book each week.**

   ______________________________ **reads a new book each week.**

5. **That flower has beautiful colors.**

   ______________________________ **has beautiful colors.**

6. **My mom and dad are going out to dinner.**

   ______________________________ **are going out to dinner.**

Name ______________________________

A **pronoun** is a word that can take the place of a noun. *I, you, he, she, it, we*, and *they* are **subject pronouns**.

Examples: **Dad** works at a television station.
He works at a television station.

The station is an exciting place to work.
It is an exciting place to work.

Change each sentence by using a pronoun in place of the underlined words.

1. <u>My family</u> just took my sister to college.

   ______________________ just took my sister to college.

2. <u>My sister</u> finished high school last year.

   ______________________ finished high school last year.

3. Now <u>Sis</u> wants to study to be a journalist.

   Now ______________________ wants to study to be a journalist.

4. <u>Mom and Dad</u> helped Sis get ready for college.

   ______________________ helped Sis get ready for college.

5. <u>A scholarship</u> will help Sis to pay for her studies.

   ______________________ will help Sis to pay for her studies.

6. Yesterday, <u>Sis and I</u> got to see the dorm where she will live.

   Yesterday, ______________________ got to see the dorm where she will live.

7. <u>The room</u> was small, but cozy.

   ______________________ was small, but cozy.

Name ______________________________ **Object Pronouns**

A **pronoun** is a word that can take the place of a noun. *Me, him, her, it, us, you*, and *them* are **object pronouns**.

Examples: Vince threw **the ball**. Vince threw **it.**
The dog licked **Kim**. The dog licked **her**.

Change each sentence by using a pronoun in place of the underlined words.

1. **Gary got <u>a camera</u> for Christmas.**

   Gary got ______________________________ for Christmas.

2. **He took a whole roll of <u>pictures</u> in one day.**

   He took a whole roll of ______________________________ in one day.

3. **One picture showed <u>Mom</u> cooking pancakes.**

   One picture showed ______________________________ cooking pancakes.

4. **Then he took a picture of <u>Lucy and me</u>.**

   Then he took a picture of ______________________________.

5. **Gary took <u>the film</u> to be developed the next day.**

   Gary took ______________________________ to be developed the next day.

Write a sentence for each of the pronouns given.

1. **him** ____

2. **them** ____

3. **me** ____

4. **us** ____

Name ______________________________ **Object Pronouns**

A **pronoun** is a word that can take the place of a noun. *Me, him, her, it, us, you*, and *them* are **object pronouns**.

Examples:

Peggy helped **Jake**.	Peggy helped **him**.
We ate **pretzels**.	We ate **them**.
Peggy phoned **Toni and Mac**.	Peggy phoned **them**.

Change each sentence by using a pronoun in place of the underlined words.

1. **Peggy called <u>Toni</u> yesterday.**

   Peggy called ______________________ yesterday.

2. **Peggy invited <u>Toni and her brother</u> to go swimming in her pool.**

   Peggy invited ______________________ to go swimming in her pool.

3. **Toni threw <u>the phone</u> down.**

   Toni threw ______________________ down.

4. **She and her brother put <u>their bathing suits</u> on quickly.**

   She and her brother put ______________________ on quickly.

5. **Their mom drove <u>the car</u> to Peggy's house.**

   Their mom drove ______________________ to Peggy's house.

6. **The kids played <u>water games</u> all day.**

   The kids played ______________________ all day.

7. **Toni and Peggy taught <u>Toni's brother</u> how to dive.**

   Toni and Peggy taught ______________________ how to dive.

8. **"Peggy is so nice to share <u>this pool</u> with us," said Toni.**

   Peggy is so nice to share ______________________ with us.

Name ______________________________

Possessive Pronouns

These **possessive pronouns** come right before nouns and show ownership: *my, his, her, its, our, your*, and *their*.

Example: Abigail's room is pink. Her room is pink.

These **possessive pronouns** are used alone: *mine, his, hers, its, ours, yours*, and *theirs*.

Example: That is Abigail's stuffed bear. That is hers.

Replace the underlined word in each sentence with the correct possessive pronoun.

1. **Toady is the family's frog.**

   Toady is ______________________ frog.

2. **Toady's collar is red.**

   ______________________ collar is red.

3. **The collar's inscription says "123 Hickory Street."**

   ______________________ inscription says "123 Hickory Street."

4. **That big fish tank is Toady's home.**

   That big fish tank is ______________________ home.

5. **Sometimes Toady eats the fishes' food.**

   Sometimes Toady eats ______________________ food.

Rewrite each sentence replacing the underlined words with a possessive pronoun.

1. **That frog is our frog.** ______________________________________

2. **This frog is my frog.** ______________________________________

Name ______________________________ **Possessive Pronouns**

These **possessive pronouns** come right before nouns and show ownership: *my, his, her, its, our, your*, and *their*.

Example: **The players' uniforms** are blue. **Their** uniforms are blue.

These **possessive pronouns** are used alone: *mine, his, hers, its, ours, yours*, and *theirs*.

Example: That is **Harry's uniform**. That is **his**.

Replace the underlined word in each sentence with the correct possessive pronoun.

1. **The Pilgrims' ship was called the *Mayflower*.**

   ______________________________ ship was called the *Mayflower*.
2. **Christopher Columbus's biggest ship was the *Santa Maria*.**

   ______________________________ biggest ship was the *Santa Maria*.
3. **Penelope is the nickname of my grandma's car.**

   Penelope is the nickname of ______________________________ car.
4. **My toy airplane's name is *King of the Sky*.**

   ______________________________ name is *King of the Sky*.
5. **The *Spirit of St. Louis* was the name of Charles Lindbergh's airplane.**

   The *Spirit of St. Louis* was the name of ______________________________ airplane.

Rewrite each sentence replacing each underlined word with a possessive pronoun.

1. **That rocket is Tony's. ______________________________**

2. **That is the astronaut's rocket. ______________________________**

Name ______________________________

Verbs are action words. They tell what a person or thing is doing.

Examples: My mom **sews** pretty clothes. Dad **builds** furniture.

Circle the verb in each sentence.

1. Kimberly's class gave a talent show.
2. Ricky played his tuba.
3. Connie sang her favorite song.
4. Derrick told jokes.
5. David and Donald did magic tricks.
6. Sandy danced the Cha-cha.

Complete each sentence with a verb from the word bank.

1. A talent is something you naturally ______________________ well.
2. Everyone ______________________ talents.
3. Some people ______________________ and paint beautiful pictures.
4. Others ______________________ sports and games well.
5. Some people ______________________ with beautiful voices.
6. Chefs ______________________ their talent to cook nice meals.

WORD BANK						
use	play	has	know	sing	do	draw

Name ______________________________

Verbs are action words. They tell what a person or thing is doing.

Examples: Mike **exercises** every day. He **eats** healthy foods. Our eyes **help** us to see. Our bones **give** our bodies shape.

Circle the verb in each sentence.

1. Your body works hard every minute of the day.
2. Your heart pumps blood with oxygen and nutrients to your cells.
3. Lungs filter oxygen from the air.
4. Your stomach breaks down food into smaller parts.
5. Muscles and joints work together to help you move.
6. Your brain controls your body's work.

Complete each sentence with a verb from the word bank.

1. Skin is a covering that ______________________ our bodies.
2. Skin ______________________ out dirt and germs.
3. Nerves in your skin help you ______________________ things like pain or cold.
4. When our bodies are too hot, we ______________________ from openings in our skin.
5. Our bodies ______________________ down when the sweat evaporates.

WORD BANK						
sweat	wear	protects	feel	cool	hurts	keeps

Name ______________________________ **Linking Verbs**

The verb **to be** is a special kind of verb called a **linking verb**. Instead of showing action, **to be** links the subject of the sentence to the rest of the sentence and tells us something about or describes the subject. Here are some forms of **to be** in the present tense:

Singular	Plural
(I) am	(we) are
(you) are	(you) are
(He, she, it) is	(they) are

Examples: I am in the fourth grade.
Chicago is a big city.
My parents are smart.

Complete each sentence with the correct form of the verb to be.

1. **A group of baby kittens ______________________ a litter.**
2. **Kittens ______________________ blind and helpless when they are born.**
3. **The mother cat ______________________ aware that her kittens need help.**
4. **She ______________________ gentle as she cares for them.**
5. **Kittens ______________________ ready to open their eyes in 10-14 days.**
6. **They ______________________ able to see especially well at night.**
7. **Kittens ______________________ also good at balancing and can move quickly.**
8. **I ______________________ so glad that I have a kitten!**

Name ________________________________ **Linking Verbs**

The verb **to be** is a special kind of verb called a **linking verb**. Instead of showing action, **to be** links the subject of the sentence to the rest of the sentence and tells us something about or describes the subject. Here are some forms of **to be** in the past tense:

Singular	Plural
(I) was	(we) were
(you) were	(you) were
(he, she, it) was	(they) were

Examples:

I was on vacation last week.
My dad was our tour guide.
Mom and Sis were our map readers.

Complete the sentences with past tense forms of to be.

1. **The coast of Oregon ______________________ a great place to visit.**
2. **The mountain cliffs ______________________ amazing.**
3. **The beach ______________________ covered with sand and shells.**
4. **Baby seals ______________________ out on the sand bars with their mothers.**
5. **Tide pools ______________________ filled with starfish and sea urchins.**
6. **In the distance, a whale ______________________ swimming in the ocean.**
7. **The ocean ______________________ too cold to swim in, but we didn't care.**
8. **We really ______________________ sad when it was time to leave the Oregon coast.**

Name ______________________________ **Helping Verbs**

Helping verbs are sometimes used with action verbs. Here is a list of common helping verbs:

am	were	shall	should	must
is	has	will	would	do
are	have	can	could	did
was	had	may	might	does

Examples: I **am** going on a trip. We **might** see a moose.

Use a helping verb from the word bank to complete each sentence.

1. **The Browns ______________________ getting ready for their vacation.**
2. **"We ______________________ take our coats," said Mrs. Brown.**
3. **"It ______________________ be cold in the mountains."**
4. **Scott ______________________ excited.**
5. **Mr. Brown ______________________ said he wants to take us hiking.**
6. **"We ______________________ see some bears in the mountains!" exclaimed little Amy.**
7. **"We ______________________ look for animals," replied mom.**
8. **"I ______________________ hoping that we see some."**
9. **"We ______________________ come here again soon!" said Mr. Brown.**

WORD BANK

will	**were**	**would**	**had**	**am**
should	**was**	**can**	**might**	**must**

Name ______________________________

Helping verbs are sometimes used with action verbs. Here is a list of common helping verbs:

am	were	shall	should	must
is	has	will	would	do
are	have	can	could	did
was	had	may	might	does

Examples: It **has** snowed all night. School **will be** canceled.

Complete each sentence with a helping verb from the list above. Some sentences may have more than one correct answer.

1. **I ______________________ eat broccoli for dinner.**
2. **I ______________________ going to ask for corn tomorrow.**
3. **I think Mom ______________________ cook macaroni and cheese too.**
4. **Dad ______________________ like that.**
5. **The best dinner ______________________ be pizza and ice cream.**

Use the verb pairs listed to write your own sentences.

1. **might go** ____

   ____
2. **was sleeping** ____

   ____
3. **have stopped** ____

   ____

Name ________________________________ **Past Tense Verbs**

To tell something that has already happened, **-ed** is added to most verbs. This form of the verb is called the **past tense**.

Examples: My friends and I play outside a lot.
Yesterday, we played outside for three hours.

Rewrite each sentence in the past tense. The first one has been done for you.

1. **I need a snack.** ***I needed a snack.***
2. **I like cold milk.** ________________________________
3. **The cookies look good.** ________________________________
4. **The snack tastes great.** ________________________________
5. **My dog plays with dirt.** ________________________________
6. **He chews on his bone.** ________________________________
7. **I laugh at his tricks.** ________________________________

Complete the sentences below using the past tense.

1. **Yesterday morning I** ________________________________.
2. **In the afternoon I** ________________________________.
3. **I** ________________________________ **last night.**
4. **I** ________________________________ **before I went to sleep.**
5. **Joe** ________________________________ **the broken pedal on his bicycle.**

Name ______________________________ **Past Tense Verbs**

To tell something that already happened, **-ed** is added to most verbs. This form of the verb is called the **past tense**.

Examples: My friends and I play outside a lot.
Yesterday we played outside for three hours.

Use the word bank to complete the past tense sentences below.

1. Timmy opened his mouth and ______________________.
2. The baby ______________________ for her bottle.
3. Marlene ______________________ her popcorn.
4. Bob ______________________ out the door an hour ago.
5. Gary ______________________ with his toy during the show.

WORD BANK				
spilled	walked	played	screamed	yawned

Rewrite each sentence below, changing it to the past tense.

1. Don and Cal want to go to the movies. ______________________

____

2. They ask their parents. ______________________

____

3. The two boys walk to the neighborhood theater. ______________________

____

Name ______________________________

Irregular Past Tense Verbs

Some verbs do not form the past tense by adding -d or -ed. They form the past tense in other ways. These verbs are called **irregular verbs**.

Examples:	I eat pizza every day.	I ate pizza last night.
	Mary buys candy at the store.	Mary bought candy yesterday.

Draw lines to match the present and past tense verb forms.

GROUP 1

take	**threw**
give	**went**
choose	**took**
throw	**rode**
go	**chose**
ride	**gave**

GROUP 2

write	**swam**
drink	**ran**
bring	**drank**
come	**wrote**
swim	**came**
run	**brought**

Use past tense verbs from the above lists to complete each sentence.

1. **We ______________________ my little brother to the zoo.**
2. **He ______________________ along his stuffed bear.**
3. **First we all ______________________ the zoo train.**
4. **Then we ______________________ to the monkey house.**
5. **We ______________________ peanuts to the monkeys.**
6. **Next we saw some seals who ______________________ in a big pool.**
7. **My friend said "Let's race," so we ______________________ to the snack bar.**

Name ________________________________

Irregular Past Tense Verbs

Some verbs do not form the past tense by adding -d or -ed. They form the past tense in other ways. These verbs are called **irregular verbs**.

Examples:	I wear shorts in summer.	I wore shorts yesterday.
	Jim sells candy bars.	Jim sold three candy bars.

Draw lines to match the present and past tense verb forms.

GROUP 1	
fall	**told**
go	**knew**
break	**fell**
sit	**went**
know	**sat**
tell	**broke**

GROUP 2	
make	**began**
eat	**felt**
think	**ate**
begin	**forgave**
feel	**made**
forgive	**thought**

Use past tense verbs from the above lists to complete the story.

When I babysat my sister, I ____________________ we would have a fun day. The day ____________________ fine. Then things got worse. My sister ____________________ down on the sidewalk. Then I ____________________ her piece of chalk accidentally. I ____________________ bad. I ____________________ my sister that I was sorry and she ____________________ me. Then, we ____________________ into the house and watched a movie.

Name ______________________________ **Verb Review**

In each blank, write the past tense form of the verbs to complete the story.

The camera was ______________________ (invent) in the 1800s. A French scientist ______________________ (take) the first photograph in 1826. Cameras ______________________ (improve) over the next 50 years, but only a few people ______________________ (have) their own cameras. Then an inventor named George Eastman ______________________ (have) an idea. He ______________________ (produce) a simple, less-expensive camera and ______________________ (sell) it to ordinary people. Many people ______________________ (buy) Eastman's camera. After they ______________________ (take) a roll of film, they ______________________ (send) it to Eastman's company where workers ______________________ (develop) it. Eastman's company ______________________ (say), "You press the button, we do the rest."

Write your own sentences about a camera, using these past tense verbs.

1. flashed ______________________________
2. clicked ______________________________
3. took ______________________________

Name ______________________________ Verb Review

The words below are all verbs. Circle every one that you have already done today. Then underline every one that you think you will do later today.

BRUSH	DRINK	WALK	THINK	FIX
EAT	DRIVE	RIDE	WAKE	KICK
DRESS	CLIMB	BOUNCE	FORGET	CRY
LAUGH	WRITE	MAKE	COOK	READ
BAKE	SKATE	REST	PRAY	HOLD
SING	CALL	FROWN	GIVE	HUG
USE	SMILE	JUMP	STAND	PAY
WAVE	TALK	PAINT	STUDY	SLEEP

Think of two OTHER verbs that you have done today.

______________________________ ______________________________

Answer these verb riddles:

I am something you might do when you are sad. What verb am I?

____

I am something a dog does to make noise. What verb am I?

____

I am what you are doing when you go off a board into the swimming pool. What verb am I?

____

Name ______________________________ **Recognizing Adjectives**

An **adjective** is a word that describes a noun. Adjectives tell facts like *what kind, which one, how much,* or *how many.*

Examples: What kind: tall mountain, red shirt, ripe fruit, short nap
Which one: Boston Harbor, this boy, these books, the other game
How much/How many: two grapes, few answers, many bugs, no gum

Circle the adjective that describes each underlined noun in the sentences below.

1. **An important statue stands in New York Harbor.**
2. **This statue was a gift to the United States from France.**
3. **It was built by a young sculptor named Auguste Bartholdi.**
4. **The United States built the big pedestal on which the statue stands.**
5. **Together the statue and the pedestal are a monument to freedom for the two nations.**
6. **It took over two hundred crates to ship the huge statue from France to New York.**
7. **Today many people still visit this famous statue.**
8. **What is this monument's name? The Statue of Liberty!**

Rewrite the sentences below, adding an adjective to describe each underlined noun. (Example: A boat took us to the statue. A big boat took us to the incredible Statue.)

1. **The statue is on the island.** ______________________________

____

2. **My family went inside the statue.** ______________________________

____

Name ______________________________ **Recognizing Adjectives**

An **adjective** is a word that describes a noun. Adjectives tell facts like *what kind, which one, how much,* or *how many.*

Examples: What kind: deep ocean, white coat, heavy rocks, quick trip
Which one: Italian food, this cat, these flowers, final race
How much/How many: two grapes, a few trees, many bugs, no gum

Circle the adjective that describes each underlined noun in the sentences below. (Hint: A few nouns have more than one adjective—can you find them?)

1. **Have you ever wondered what materials make up our amazing Earth?**
2. **The first layer inside Earth is called the crust.**
3. **The hard, rocky crust is like a shell around the Earth.**
4. **Underneath the crust are three layers of rocks and metals.**
5. **The mantle is 1,800 miles thick and is made of heavy rocks.**
6. **In some places, the mantle is so hot that the rocks melt!**
7. **The next layer of Earth is the outer core.**
8. **The outer core contains hot, melted rock.**
9. **The inner core is at the center of Earth.**
10. **Two types of metal, iron and nickel, make up the solid core.**

Rewrite the sentences below, adding an adjective to describe each underlined noun.

1. **Earth is a planet.** ______________________________

____

2. **Scientists study Earth.** ______________________________

____

Name ________________________________ **Recognizing Adjectives**

An **adjective** is a word that describes a noun. Adjectives tell facts like *what kind, which one, how much,* or *how many*.

Examples: What kind: friendly girl, green tree, cold ice cream
Which one: that car, those videos, last game
How much/How many: five bees, few bites, some toes, no mice

Write an adjective to describe each noun. Then write a sentence using both nouns and their adjectives.

1. ______________________ **mother** ______________________ **vegetables**

____

2. ______________________ **airplane** ______________________ **children**

____

3. ______________________ **bear** ______________________ **forest**

____

4. ______________________ **hat** ______________________ **man**

____

5. ______________________ **book** ______________________ **page**

____

6. ______________________ **face** ______________________ **smile**

____

7. ______________________ **room** ______________________ **floor**

____

Name ______________________________ **Recognizing Adjectives**

An **adjective** is a word that describes a noun. Adjectives tell facts like *what kind, which one, how much,* or *how many.*

Examples: What kind: The shiny, metal object looked like gold!
Which one: These pieces of metal are gold!
How much/How many: This gold is worth a thousand dollars!

In the paragraph below, circle the adjectives that describe each underlined noun.

How the Gold Rush Began

In 1848 a young carpenter named James Marshall made an important discovery that sent many Americans rushing to California. On January 24th, Marshall stopped his carpentry work to take a quiet walk along the river. Looking into the clear, blue water, Marshall saw a shiny, yellow object. As he bent down, he saw more gleaming objects. Marshall felt the soft metal. Could this be gold? He ran to tell his boss, John Sutter. What Marshall had found that day was gold. With his exciting discovery, the California Gold Rush began.

Complete the story using your own adjectives.

I love my ______________________ puppy. We bought him at the ______________________ store in the mall. His eyes are ______________________, his fur is ______________________, and his ears are ______________________. He loves to run across our ______________________ yard. We have ______________________ of fun together.

Name ______________________________

Words that describe (tell more about) people, places, and things are called **adjectives**. Sometimes adjectives come after the noun they describe, usually after linking verbs like *am, is, are, was,* and *were*.

Examples: I am sleepy. My parents are kind. The grass is tall. John was happy.

Underline the adjectives in the sentences below. Circle the noun they describe. The first one has been done for you.

1. **(Herman) is huge and hairy.**
2. **The saleslady was polite.**
3. **Those brownies are delicious.**
4. **My grandparents are loving and kind.**
5. **Yesterday the clouds were big and puffy.**
6. **I was surprised by my party.**
7. **I am hungry.**
8. **The tulips are yellow and red.**

Use the two adjectives listed below in a sentence. Write the sentence so that the adjectives come after the verb. The first one has been done for you.

1. **tall and green** ***The fir trees were tall and green.***
2. **quiet and peaceful** ______________________________
3. **long and wide** ______________________________
4. **large and yellow** ______________________________

Name ______________________ **Adjective Comparison**

To compare two nouns, use the comparative form of the adjective. This is formed by adding **-er** to most adjectives. When using adjectives of three or more syllables, you can usually add the word **more** before the adjective.
To compare three or more nouns, use the superlative form of the adjective. This is formed by adding **-est** to most adjectives. When using adjectives of three or more syllables add the word **most** in front of the adjective.

Examples:

That silver trumpet is louder than the gold one.
It is the loudest trumpet I have ever heard.

The red dress was more beautiful than the green one.
It was the most beautiful dress I had ever seen.

Write the comparative and superlative forms of each adjective. The first one has been done for you.

Adjective	Comparative	Superlative
1. fast	**faster**	**fastest**
2. tall	______	______
3. strong	______	______
4. smart	______	______
5. generous	______	______
6. quick	______	______
7. old	______	______
8. wise	______	______
9. delicate	______	______
10. high	______	______

Name ________________________ **Adjective Comparison**

To compare two nouns, use the comparative form of the adjective. This is formed by adding **-er** to most adjectives. When using adjectives of three or more syllables, you can usually add the word **more** before the adjective.
To compare three or more nouns, use the superlative form of the adjective. This is formed by adding **-est** to most adjectives. When using adjectives of three or more syllables add the word **most** in front of the adjective.

Examples: The basket is heavier than the box.
It is the heaviest basket I've ever carried.

Dan is more courageous than Jim.
Dan is the most courageous person I know.

Circle the better sentence in each pair.

1. **The first gymnast was skillfuler than the second one.**
   The first gymnast was more skillful than the second one.

2. **Zack's yell was the loudest of all.**
   Zack's yell was the most loud of all.

3. **The big pine tree was older than the fir tree.**
   The big pine tree was more old than the fir tree.

4. **That was the incrediblest bubble I've ever blown!**
   That was the most incredible bubble I've ever blown!

5. **After the slumber party, Mary was sleepier than Leann.**
   After the slumber party, Mary was more sleepy than Leann.

6. **June was confidenter than Jane that she would pass the test.**
   June was more confident than Jane that she would pass the test.

7. **The newborn puppies were smaller than their mothers.**
   The newborn puppies were more small than their mothers.

8. **The Grand Tetons are the magnificentest mountains I have ever seen.**
   The Grand Tetons are the most magnificent mountains I have ever seen.

Name ______________________________ **Adjective Comparison**

The adjective **good** has special forms for comparison. To compare two things, the word **better** is used. To compare more than two things, the word **best** is used.

Examples: The apple pie was <u>good</u>.
The cherry pie was <u>better</u> than the apple pie.
The blueberry pie was the <u>best</u> pie of all.

The adjective **bad** has special forms for comparison also. To compare two things, the word **worse** is used. To compare more than two things the word **worst** is used.

Examples: That shampoo has a <u>bad</u> smell.
That shampoo smells <u>worse</u> than a skunk!
That is the <u>worst</u> smelling shampoo ever!

Choose the correct form of good or bad to complete each sentence.

1. **That was the ______________________ baseball game I've seen all year.**
(good / better / best)

2. **I think asparagus is ______________________ than lima beans.**
(bad / worse / worst)

3. **That camera takes the ______________________ pictures I've ever seen.**
(bad / worse / worst)

4. **Ben's skis are ______________________ than Jan's.**
(bad / worse / worst)

5. **The flu is ______________________ than a cold.**
(bad / worse / worst)

6. **The chicken pox is the ______________________ illness I've ever had.**
(bad / worse / worst)

7. **My pen is ______________________ than Mary's pen.**
(good / better / best)

8. **Nick has ______________________ shoes for soccer than Lance.**
(good / better / best)

Name ______________________________ **Articles**

Articles are small words that come before nouns or noun phrases. **A**, **an,** and **the** are articles. **A** is used before a word that begins with a consonant. **An** is used before a word that begins with a vowel. Use **the** before a noun that names a particular person, place, or thing.

Examples:

an ocean
a continent
The earth is tilted a little bit.
The weather today is warm.

Write the correct article (*a or an*) before the noun or noun phrase.

1. ______________ climate
2. ______________ igloo
3. ______________ ear
4. ______________ lamp
5. ______________ ray of sun
6. ______________ ice cube
7. ______________ satellite
8. ______________ oven

Use articles (*a, an*, or *the*) to complete each sentence.

1. There is ______________ imaginary line around ______________ center of ______________ earth that is called ______________ equator.
2. ______________ sun's rays shine most directly at ______________ equator.
3. ______________ climate is a pattern of weather in an area over ______________ period of time.
4. ______________ scientist who studies climate is ______________ climatologist.

Name ______________________________ **Adjective Review**

Find the adjective that describes the underlined noun in each sentence. Write it on the line.

______________ 1. Australia is a fascinating <u>country</u>.

______________ 2. It has a lot of <u>land</u>, but only 18 million people.

______________ 3. The aborigines were the first <u>Australians</u>.

______________ 4. The Australian <u>continent</u> is south of the equator.

______________ 5. Seasons south of the equator take place at opposite <u>times</u> of the year than they do north of the equator.

______________ 6. In Australia, people can go snow <u>skiing</u> in July.

______________ 7. They can sunbathe during our winter <u>holidays</u>.

______________ 8. Unique <u>animals</u> live in Australia's outback.

Circle the adjectives that you find in each sentence. The number tells you how many there are.

1. Tasmania is the smallest state in Australia. (1)
2. Tasmania is an island off the southern coast of Australia. (1)
3. It is a beautiful island with dense forests and wild rivers. (3)
4. Tasmania used to be a prison colony. (1)
5. Now many tourists come to this island. (2)
6. Some visitors take bushwalks to see the awesome scenery. (2)

Name ______________________________ **Recognizing Adverbs**

An **adverb** is a word that describes a verb. Adverbs tell *where, when, how,* or *to what extent* (how much or how long).

Examples:
The boat is leaving now. (When?)
My horse fell down. (Where?)
Paul worked busily. (How?)
William rode for days. (How long?)

Circle the adverb in each sentence. Underline the verb it describes.

1. **Paul Revere and William Dawes rode secretly.**
2. **The people of Lexington awoke early.**
3. **They arose quickly.**
4. **The British soldiers marched ahead.**
5. **Shots were fired somewhere.**
6. **The colonists fought bravely.**
7. **The Battle of Lexington ended quickly.**
8. **The Revolutionary War began here.**

Underline each adverb in the paragraph below. (There are six).

"The Shot Heard 'Round the World"

The British soldiers marched forward to Concord. The colonists' war supplies were stored there. The war supplies were destroyed, but the colonists fought long and hard. The British had to turn back to Boston. The Battle of Concord will be remembered forever in American history.

Name ______________________________ **Recognizing Adverbs**

An **adverb** is a word that describes a verb. Adverbs *tell where, when, how,* or *to what extent* (how much or how long).

Examples: The ticket booth opens now. (When?)
The line starts here. (Where?)
We petted the animals gently. (How?)
The baboons howled endlessly. (How long?)

Complete the sentences below, using an adverb from the adverb bank.

ADVERB BANK

When	Where	How	How much or How Long
daily	away	sloppily	often
now	down	carefully	never
usually	here	softly	forever
sometimes	nearby	secretly	far

1. **The zookeeper feeds the animals ______________________.**
2. **The monkeys eat their food ______________________.**
3. **Lions eat the grass. The vultures wait ______________________.**
4. **The zookeeper ______________________ forgets to feed the animals.**
5. **We watch ______________________ while the koala eats his bamboo.**

Write four sentences using the adverb given.

1. **(usually)** ____
2. **(here)** ____
3. **(softly)** ____
4. **(forever)** ____

Name ______________________________ **Recognizing Adverbs**

An **adverb** is a word that describes a verb. Adverbs tell *where, when, how,* or *to what extent* (how much or how long).

Examples: The 100-meter dash starts tomorrow. (When?)
That runner fell down. (Where?)
The ticket-takers worked quickly. (How?)
Marathon runners run far. (How long?)

Circle the adverb in each sentence. Underline the verb it describes.

1. **We drove excitedly to Atlanta, Georgia.**
2. **The 1996 Olympic Games were there.**
3. **At the track and field events, contestants ran fast and jumped.**
4. **Gymnasts moved gracefully.**
5. **At the swimming pool, swimmers glided swiftly through the water.**
6. **Then the divers gave a show.**
7. **They dove down into the deep water.**
8. **Maybe if I work hard, I can be in the Olympics.**

Write your own sentences about sports using the adverbs listed.

1. **carefully** ______________________________
2. **tomorrow** ______________________________
3. **outside** ______________________________
4. **quickly** ______________________________

Name ______________________________ **Recognizing Adverbs**

An **adverb** is a word that describes a verb. Adverbs tell *where, when, how,,* or *to what extent* (how much or how long).

Examples:
You can have a snack later. (When?)
Are there cookies here? (Where?)
Mom makes cookies easily. (How?)
I never eat potato chips. (How much?)

Use your imagination to complete the story with adverbs. Remember, adverbs tell when, where, how, or to what extent (how much or how long).

News travels ______________________________ in my school. On the day I won 100 ice cream cone coupons, ______________________________ everybody was my friend. Marty came ______________________________ up to me. She begged me for a chocolate cone. I told her ______________________________ that I would think about it. Fernando came ______________________________. He got ______________________________ on his knees and begged ______________________________. Jill offered to trade me her bubble gum for a strawberry ice cream coupon, but I said "No, thanks." Wow, people sure act ______________________________ sometimes. I ______________________________ do want to share my ice cream cones, I just want to wait ______________________________.

Name ______________________________ **Recognizing Adverbs**

Circle the adverb that describes the underlined verb.

1. Our class went to Funtime Park yesterday.
2. A few of the girls ran immediately to the carousel.
3. James and I rode the roller coaster first.
4. James had never ridden a roller coaster before.
5. The car climbed slowly up the track.
6. Then we plunged downward.
7. Bill and I screamed loudly.
8. You may think we really hated our ride.
9. Not at all. We rode it again!
10. This time we rode fearlessly in the front seat.

Think of an adverb to describe each verb.

ran ______________________ turned ______________________

ate ______________________ shouted ______________________

Use the verbs and adverbs from above to write four sentences.

1. ____
2. ____
3. ____
4. ____

Name ______________________________ **Parts of Speech**

Match the parts of speech you have learned with their definitions.

______ 1. Noun	A) tells what is happening in the sentence
______ 2. Verb	B) describes a verb
______ 3. Adjective	C) describes a noun
______ 4. Adverb	D) names a person, place, or thing

Find parts of speech in the sentences below and write them on the lines.

1. These berries smash easily.

   Noun ______________________ Adjective ______________________

   Verb ______________________ Adverb ______________________

2. Ten soldiers march together.

   Noun ______________________ Adjective ______________________

   Verb ______________________ Adverb ______________________

3. The big pillow belongs here.

   Noun ______________________ Adjective ______________________

   Verb ______________________ Adverb ______________________

4. Round balls bounce nicely.

   Noun ______________________ Adjective ______________________

   Verb ______________________ Adverb ______________________

Name ______________________________ **Word Order**

Changing the **order of words** in a sentence can change the meaning.

Example: *Kangaroos are bigger than elephants.*
Elephants are bigger than kangaroos.

Both sentences have the same words but in a different order.
Only one of the sentences states a fact.

For each pair of sentences below, circle the one that is correct.

1. **The Earth travels around the Sun.**
   The Sun travels around the Earth.

2. **A man becomes a boy.**
   A boy becomes a man.

3. **A coconut is bigger than a lemon.**
   A lemon is bigger than a coconut.

4. **Flowers get pollen from bees.**
   Bees get pollen from flowers.

5. **Dogs are a kind of animal.**
   Animals are a kind of dog.

6. **Horses are faster than airplanes.**
   Airplanes are faster than horses.

7. **A circle is round and a square has four sides.**
   A square is round and a circle has four sides.

8. **Apples grow on trees.**
   Trees grow on apples.

9. **The equator is north of Canada.**
   Canada is north of the equator.

10. **The Earth lived on dinosaurs long ago.**
    Dinosaurs lived on the Earth long ago.

Name ________________________________ **Statements**

A statement is a sentence that tells something. Statements begin with a capital letter and end with a period (.).

Examples of statements: The Netherlands is a beautiful country.
The Netherlands has a queen.

Not statements: What kind of money do Dutch people use?
Look at all the canals!

Write S on the line if the sentence is a statement.

________ 1. **I like to go swimming during the summer.**

________ 2. **Is your name Fred?**

________ 3. **My friend is the girl in the red shirt.**

________ 4. **Yesterday we ate pizza for dinner.**

________ 5. **Are you going to the party?**

________ 6. **Yikes, that must have hurt!**

Rewrite each statement correctly below. Remember to capitalize the first word and end each sentence with a period.

1. **my family worked in the yard all day**

____

2. **howard always tells the truth**

____

3. **soccer is a fun game**

____

Name ______________________________ **Questions**

A **question** is a sentence that asks something. A question begins with a capital letter and ends with a question mark (?).

Examples: What is your favorite sport?
Do you like to play it or watch it?

Write Q on the blank if the sentence is a question.

_______ 1. **Do you like to watch basketball games?**

_______ 2. **I think basketball games are exciting.**

_______ 3. **What is double-dribbling?**

_______ 4. **Look out for that ball!**

_______ 5. **Why are some shots worth three points?**

_______ 6. **The first basketball hoops were peach baskets hung up on a wall.**

Rewrite each question correctly below. Remember to capitalize the first word and end each sentence with a question mark.

1. **who invented basketball**

____

2. **how long does a game last**

____

3. **what is a free throw**

____

4. **where did you learn to play basketball**

____

Name ________________________________

An **exclamation** is a sentence that shows excitement or a strong feeling. An exclamation starts with a capital letter and ends with an exclamation point **(!)**. An exclamation may be only one or two words long.

Examples:	I can't believe it!	Wow, this is great!
	Look out!	It's so hot outside!

Write EX on the blank if the sentence is an exclamation.

_______ 1. **Whee, here we go!**

_______ 2. **This water slide is great!**

_______ 3. **The water at the bottom is pretty cold.**

_______ 4. **Did you try slide number three?**

_______ 5. **Wait till Ben hears about this place!**

_______ 6. **Here I go!**

Rewrite each exclamation correctly below. Remember to capitalize the first word and end each sentence with an exclamation mark.

1. **summer's finally here**

   ____

2. **hooray for you**

   ____

3. **let's go swimming**

   ____

4. **watch me dive**

   ____

Name ______________________________

Commands are sentences that tell someone to do something. Strong commands end with exclamation points **(!)**.

Examples:

Put the baby down.
I said "NO!"

Clean your room now!
Watch out!

Write each command correctly on the line. Each is a strong command.

1. **fasten your seat belt**

____

2. **be careful**

____

3. **lock the door**

____

4. **don't litter**

____

5. **try again**

____

6. **stop whining**

____

Can you think of three commands someone has given you in the last week? Write them below.

1. ______________________________

2. ______________________________

3. ______________________________

Name ________________________________ Types of Sentences Review

On the blank write S if the sentence is a statement, Q if it is a question, EX if it is an exclamation, and C if it is a command.

________ 1. Is there always this much water falling?

________ 2. What an amazing view!

________ 3. What causes a waterfall?

________ 4. These waterfalls are named Niagara Falls.

________ 5. I see a rainbow!

________ 6. Watch out!

________ 7. Niagara Falls are on the border of the United States and Canada.

________ 8. Can you see the falls from both countries?

________ 9. Stand back from the edge!

________ 10. Look at all the people!

Make your own sentences! Complete your own statement, question, exclamation, and command. Don't forget to use the correct punctuation.

1. I think ____

2. Do you ____

3. Wow, ____

4. Never____

Name ______________________________ Types of Sentences Review

On the blank write S if the sentence is a statement, Q if it is a question, EX if it is an exclamation, and C if it is a command.

________1. How big is the Sun?

________ 2. Wow, that is beautiful!

________ 3. How fast does the Earth travel around the Sun?

________ 4. The Earth is 93 million miles from the Sun.

________ 5. That's farther than I can imagine!

________ 6. Watch out—don't look directly at the Sun!

________ 7. The Sun is an enormous ball of burning gas.

________ 8. Can satellites take pictures of the Sun?

________ 9. Nothing can get too close to the Sun!

________10. Put that sun screen on now!

Make your own sentences! Complete your own statement, question, exclamation, and command. Don't forget to use the correct punctuation.

1. The Sun ____

2. Are you ____

3. Hey, ____

4. Always ____

Name ______________________________

The **subject** of a sentence tells who or what the sentence is about. The **simple subject** is the noun that the sentence is about. The **complete subject** includes the words that tell more about the subject.

Examples: **Painting and sculpting** are two forms of art.
Some sculptors model out of clay.
I like to carve wood.

Circle the simple subject. Underline the complete subject.

1. **Many painters use different styles.**
2. **One style of painting is called Impressionism.**
3. **The art called impressionism began in France around 1875.**
4. **Claude Monet is considered the first impressionist painter.**
5. **His famous paintings were full of light.**
6. **The impressionists' goal was to capture light in their pictures.**
7. **Renoir and Pissarro are other famous impressionist painters.**
8. **Mary Cassatt, a female artist, brought Impressionism to America.**
9. **This woman is especially famous for her pictures of mothers and children.**
10. **Many people enjoy the impressionists' paintings in museums.**

Write your own simple or complete subject for each sentence.

1. ______________________________ **is a wise thing to do.**
2. ______________________________ **mow the grass.**
3. ______________________________ **study for the test.**
4. ______________________________ **practice hard every day.**

Name ______________________________

The **subject** of a sentence tells who or what the sentence is about. The **simple subject** is the noun that the sentence is about. The **complete subject** includes the words that tell more about the subject.

Examples:

A *ship* with red and white sails moved across the water.
It was a Viking ship.
***Eric the Red*, a famous Viking**, captained the ship.

Circle the simple subject. Write the complete subject of the sentence on the line.

1. **A group of bold seamen lived in northern Europe 1000 years ago.**

____

2. **These men were called the Vikings.**

____

3. **The Vikings loved adventure.**

____

4. **They sailed the oceans in beautifully painted ships.**

____

5. **Eric the Red was a Viking leader.**

____

6. **He led the Vikings across the "Sea of Darkness."**

____

7. **The "Sea of Darkness" is what they called the Atlantic Ocean.**

____

8. **These seamen sailed to Iceland and then to Greenland.**

____

Name ___________________________ **Predicates**

The **predicate** is the part of a sentence that tells something about the subject. The **simple predicate** is the verb. The **complete predicate** includes words that tell more about the verb.

Examples: The earth **has seven continents.**
The United States **is in North America**.

Circle the simple predicate. Write the complete predicate on the line.

1. **The largest continent is Asia.**

   ____

2. **Russia, China, and India are in Asia.**

   ____

3. **Europe is connected to Asia.**

   ____

4. **Europe is the smallest continent.**

   ____

5. **Some continents have many countries.**

   ____

6. **Australia is a continent and a country.**

   ____

7. **Many small countries are on the continent of Africa.**

   ____

Complete each sentence by writing your own predicate.

1. **One continent** ___________________________

2. **Antarctica** ___________________________

Name ______________________________

The **predicate** is the part of a sentence that tells something about the subject. The **simple predicate** is the verb. The **complete predicate** includes words that tell more about the verb.

Examples: The Middle Ages ***happened*** **1000 years ago**.
It ***was*** **the time of knights and noblemen**.

Circle the simple predicate. Underline the complete predicate.

1. **People in Europe long ago lived on manors.**
2. **A manor was the land that belonged to a nobleman.**
3. **The nobleman ruled all of the people on his land.**
4. **A rich nobleman might have a castle on his land.**
5. **Castles were cold, damp, and dark.**
6. **There was also much farmland on a manor.**
7. **Peasants were the people who farmed the nobleman's land.**
8. **Peasants worked very hard.**
9. **They lived in small huts with dirt floors.**
10. **No peasants could read or write.**
11. **Very few noblemen learned to read or write.**

Complete each sentence by writing your own predicate.

1. **The life of a nobleman** ______________________________
2. **The life of a peasant** ______________________________
3. **I** ______________________________

Name ______________________________ **Subjects & Predicates**

Every sentence has two parts: the subject and the predicate. The subject tells who or what the sentence is about. The predicate tells something about the subject.

Examples: My grandpa works in his garden every day.
Subject Predicate
Tulips and daffodils are blooming in his yard.
Subject Predicate

Match each subject on the left with a predicate on the right to make a complete sentence. Write the sentences below.

SUBJECTS	**PREDICATES**
The pink rose	**is Mrs. Payne.**
Last night's thunderstorm	**smells wonderful.**
My teacher's name	**scared my little sister.**
Milton	**is our mailman.**

1. ______________________________

2. ______________________________

3. ______________________________

4. ______________________________

Write your own subject to complete each sentence below.

1. ______________________ **eats pancakes and sausage every day.**

2. ______________________ **like biscuits and jam.**

Write your own predicate to complete each sentence below.

1. Jack and Jill ______________________.

2. Little Red Riding Hood ______________________.

Name ________________________________ **Subjects & Predicates**

Every sentence has two parts: the subject and the predicate. The subject tells who or what the sentence is about. The predicate tells something about the subject.

Examples:

Camping is fun when there are no bugs.
Subject — Predicate

The big owls hooted all night long.
Subject — Predicate

In each sentence below, underline the complete subject once and the complete predicate twice.

1. **Dad and I took our first camping trip.**
2. **We had a great time.**
3. **Our tent was just the right size.**
4. **Swimming and fishing kept us busy.**
5. **Our campfire burned brightly.**
6. **Dad told me stories about his boyhood.**
7. **The mosquitoes weren't too bad.**
8. **Two raccoons tried to eat our food.**

Write your own subject to complete each sentence below.

1. ______________________________ **made a lot of noise at night.**
2. ______________________________ **ate our popcorn.**

Write your own predicate to complete each sentence below.

1. **A grizzly bear** ______________________________.
2. **The other campers** ______________________________.

Name ______________________________ **Combining Subjects**

When two short sentences have the same verb, you can combine the subjects with the word *and*. This makes one longer, more interesting sentence.

Examples: **Thomas Edison** was a great inventor.
Guglielmo Marconi was a great inventor.
Thomas Edison and Guglielmo Marconi were great inventors.

Combine the subjects in each pair of sentences. Write the new sentence on the line.

1. **Automobiles were great inventions. Airplanes were great inventions.**

   ____

2. **Charles Duryea experimented with cars. Henry Ford experimented with cars.**

   ____

3. **The Model T was an early car. The Model A was an early car.**

   ____

4. **New roads were built for cars. New bridges were built for cars.**

   ____

5. **Orville Wright invented the airplane. Wilbur Wright invented the airplane.**

   ____

6. **Charles Lindbergh was a famous pilot. Amelia Earhart was a famous pilot.**

   ____

7. **The automobile made travel faster and easier. The airplane made travel faster and easier.**

   ____

Name ______________________________ **Combining Subjects**

When two short sentences have the same verb, you can combine the subjects with the word *and*. This makes one longer, more interesting sentence.

Example: **Pumice** is a type of rock.
Basalt is a type of rock.
Pumice and basalt are types of rock.

Use the words given to make one sentence that has two subjects. The first one has been done for you.

1. **cars, trains** *Cars and trains are both fun ways to travel.* ____________

____

2. **airplanes, rockets** ______________________________

____

3. **stones, pebbles** ______________________________

____

4. **dogs, cats** ______________________________

____

5. **table, chairs** ______________________________

____

6. **trees, flowers** ______________________________

____

7. **wind, rain** ______________________________

____

Name ______________________________ **Combining Predicates**

When two short sentences have the same subject, but different verbs, you can combine the verbs with the word *and* or *but*. This makes one longer, more interesting sentence.

Examples:

Many inventors work hard.
Many inventors never become famous.
Many inventors work hard but never become famous.

Combine the predicates in each pair of sentences with the word given (*and* or *but*). Write the new sentence on the line.

1. **Thomas Edison was a school dropout. Thomas Edison became a great inventor. (but)**

   ____

2. **Young Edison worked as a telegraph operator. Young Edison planned his inventions. (and)**

   ____

3. **Edison built his own laboratory. Edison hired some assistants. (and)**

   ____

4. **Edison invented the record player. Edison perfected the electric light. (and)**

   ____

5. **Edison invented the voting machine. Edison invented the microphone. (and)**

   ____

6. **Edison did not invent television. Edison's discoveries helped make television possible. (but)**

   ____

Name ______________________________ **Combining Predicates**

When two short sentences have the same subject, but different verbs, you can combine the verbs with the word *and* or *but.* This makes one longer, more interesting sentence.

Examples: Turtles **live in water**.
Turtles **lay their eggs on land**.
Turtles **live in water but lay their eggs on land**.

Combine the predicates in each pair of sentences with the word given (*and* or *but*). Write the new sentence on the line.

1. **Anteaters eat bugs. Anteaters don't have any teeth. (but)**

   ____

2. **I like to ride my bike. I like to go for walks. (and)**

   ____

3. **Molly loves the summer. Molly does not like the winter. (but)**

   ____

4. **The days are long in the summer. The days are short in the winter. (and)**

   ____

5. **My house has four bedrooms. My house has two swimming pools. (and)**

   ____

6. **Sometimes I don't like to study. I like to make good grades. (but)**

   ____

Name ____________________ **Combining Sentences**

Sometimes two short sentences about the same topic can be combined into one more interesting sentence. Combine the sentences with a comma (,) and the words *and* or *but.*

Example: Trees shade our yards. They give us beauty.
Trees shade our yards, and they give us beauty.

Combine the two sentences using a comma and the word *and* or *but.* Write the new sentence on the line. The first one has been done for you.

1. **Trees have many parts. They are all important.**

   Trees have many parts, and they are all important.

2. **Roots anchor the tree to the ground. They take water from the soil.**

   ____

3. **The trunk supports the tree. It gives the tree strength.**

   ____

4. **Some tree trunks are straight. Some are twisted.**

   ____

5. **Branches give the tree shape. They hold the leaves out to the sun.**

   ____

6. **Leaves are where the tree makes its food. Flowers are where the seeds grow.**

   ____

7. **Some trees have big flowers. Others have flowers that are hard to see.**

   ____

8. **Some seeds are protected by cones. Others are protected by fruit.**

   ____

Name ________________________________

Sometimes two short sentences about the same topic can be combined into one more interesting sentence. Combine the sentences with a comma (,) and the words *and* or *but*.

Example: We saw many mushrooms. We didn't pick them.
We saw many mushrooms, but we didn't pick them.

Combine the two sentences using a comma and the word *and* or *but*. Write the new sentence on the line. The first one has been done for you.

1. **There are many kinds of mushrooms. Only some are edible.**

   There are many kinds of mushrooms, but only some are edible.

2. **Some mushrooms grow in meadows. Some grow on tree stumps.**

   ____

3. **Some mushrooms taste sweet. Some are very peppery tasting.**

   ____

4. **Many people eat mushrooms in salads. They can also be cooked.**

   ____

5. **Most poisonous mushrooms grow in the woods. They are sometimes hard to recognize.**

   ____

6. **A mushroom is a fungus. It feeds on other organisms.**

   ____

7. **Some mushrooms can be poisonous. Only trained collectors should gather them.**

   ____

Name ________________________________ **Subject-Verb Agreement**

Verbs that are in the **present tense** (tell what is happening now) have two forms. Use the form that goes with the subject. When the subject is third person singular (he, she, it, Mary, the dog, Joe) the verb usually ends in **-s**.

Examples: Jed runs. The dog barks.

When the subject is not third person singular (I, you, we, they, the people) **-s** is usually not added.

Examples: They run. Fido and Rover bark.

Complete each sentence with the correct verb form.

1. **In the summer, I ______________________ as a detective.**
   (work / works)
2. **I ______________________ neighborhood mysteries.**
   (solve / solves)
3. **When Mrs. Carter ______________________ her cat, I help her find it.**
   (lose / loses)
4. **If there are footprints, I ______________________ out whose they are.**
   (find / finds)
5. **My friend Jim ______________________ me secret messages.**
   (write / writes)
6. **I ______________________ my decoder to figure them out.**
   (use / uses)
7. **I ______________________ my detective kit in a secret place.**
   (keep / keeps)
8. **Only Mom and Dad ______________________ where it is.**
   (know / knows)
9. **Jim ______________________ to be a neighborhood detective too.**
   (want / wants)
10. **Then we can ______________________ mysteries together.**
    (solve / solves)

Name ______________________________ **Subject-Verb Agreement**

Complete each sentence with the correct verb form.

1. **Sound is what you** ______________________ **when air**
(hear / hears)
______________________ **back and forth quickly, or**
(move / moves)
______________________.
(vibrate / vibrates)

2. **All musical instruments** ______________________ **sound, but they**
(make / makes)
______________________ **it in different ways.**
(make / makes)

3. **When you** ______________________ **a piano key, a string**
(press / presses)
______________________ **to make sound.**
(vibrate / vibrates)

4. **A guitar player** ______________________ **strings to make sound.**
(strum / strums)

5. **A wind instrument** ______________________ **sound when someone**
(make / makes)
______________________ **into it.**
(blow / blows)

6. **To make a trumpet sound, the musician** ______________________
(blow / blows)
into the instrument and ______________________ **buttons.**
(push / pushes)

7. **Drums** ______________________ **sound when someone**
(make / makes)
______________________ **them.**
(strike / strikes)

Name ________________________________ **Sentence Fragments**

A sentence is a group of words that tells a complete idea. A sentence begins with a capital letter and ends with a punctuation mark. When a sentence is left incomplete it is called a **fragment**.

Examples:	Sentence	There are many kinds of storms.
	Fragment	Kinds of storms.
	Sentence	Storms can be very powerful.
	Fragment	Can be very powerful.

Write S if the words below are a sentence and F if they are a fragment.

_______ 1. **Blowing wildly and knocking down trees.**

_______ 2. **Lightning is a spark of electricity in the sky.**

_______ 3. **A very loud noise.**

_______ 4. **Thunder is a noise made when hot and cold air meet.**

_______ 5. **Powerful windstorm.**

_______ 6. **A tornado is shaped like a funnel.**

_______ 7. **Hurricanes are storms that start over oceans.**

_______ 8. **Called the eye of the storm.**

_______ 9. **Hurricanes are also called typhoons.**

_______10. **Extreme weather conditions.**

Add words of your own to make each phrase a sentence.

1. **Rain storms are** ____

2. **Lightning** ____

Name ______________________________ **Sentence Fragments**

Write S if the words below are a sentence and F if they are a fragment.

________ 1. There are many beautiful mountain ranges in the world.

________ 2. The highest mountain chain is the Himalayas.

________ 3. Stretch across much of Asia.

________ 4. The Swiss and Austrian Alps have many wildflowers.

________ 5. Perhaps the most famous mountains in the world.

________ 6. Mont Blanc is Europe's highest mountain.

________ 7. The Rocky Mountains and the Appalachian Mountains.

________ 8. The Rockies run through western Canada and the United States.

________ 9. Called the Appalachian Trail.

_______ 10. Mountains are a majestic, awesome sight.

Underline the fragments in the paragraph below.

In 1953 a group of explorers set off. To climb Mount Everest. Mount Everest is the world's highest mountain. Standing at 8,848 meters high. Edmund Hillary of New Zealand and Tenzing Norgay of Nepal were the only two men to reach the mountain's top. They edged up the final ice-covered rock on May 29, 1953. Stood at the top of the world.

Name ______________________________

Direct Objects

A noun or a pronoun that receives the action of the verb is called a **direct object**. Direct objects follow action verbs and answer the questions "What?" or "Whom?"

Examples: My family watched the sunset. (Watched what?)
I like my grandmother. (Like whom?)
I like her. (Like whom?)

Circle the verb in each sentence. Then find the direct object and write it on the line. (Hint: When you find the verb, ask yourself the questions "What?" or "Whom?") The first one has been done for you.

farm **1. Uncle John owns a farm.**

______________ **2. Every day he milks the cows.**

______________ **3. He plants corn in the spring.**

______________ **4. Uncle John feeds the pigs.**

______________ **5. He takes his horses to shows.**

______________ **6. Aunt Vivian grows vegetables.**

______________ **7. She cans tomatoes every summer.**

______________ **8. She also bakes bread.**

Complete each sentence by writing your own direct objects.

1. **The horses eat ______________.**
2. **The kittens drink ______________.**
3. **I saw ______________ on the farm.**
4. **The children help plant ______________.**

Name ______________________________

A noun or a pronoun that receives the action of the verb is called a **direct object**. Direct objects follow action verbs and answer the questions "What?" or "Whom?"

Examples: I drove the car to the airport. (Drove what?)
I visited Uncle Pedro. (Visited whom?)
I like him. (Like whom?)

Circle the verb in each sentence. Then find the direct object and write it on the line. (Hint: When you find the verb, ask yourself the questions "What?" or "Whom?") The first one has been done for you.

______________________ **1. In Mexico City you will see many people.**

______________________ **2. Cars and buses crowd the streets.**

______________________ **3. You may breathe smog there.**

______________________ **4. You can also see beautiful sights.**

______________________ **5. You can eat tacos.**

______________________ **6. You may even see a bullfight.**

______________________ **7. You can buy a sombrero for your head.**

______________________ **8. Many tourists visit Aztec ruins.**

Complete each sentence by writing your own direct objects.

1. I would like to visit ______________________.

2. I would see ______________________.

3. I might find ______________________.

4. I would eat ______________________.

Name ________________________________ Word Usage

ITS AND IT'S

Its is a possessive pronoun and does not have an apostrophe.

Example: That is my dog. Its fur is brown.

It's is a contraction for *it is* or *it has* and has an apostrophe.

Examples: It's a warm day today. (It is a warm day today.)
It's taken a long time. (It has taken a long time.)

Complete each sentence with either *its* or *it's*.

1. **My kitty chased ________________________ tail.**
2. **________________________ almost time for the bell to ring.**
3. **The grizzly bear was looking for ________________________ cub.**
4. **________________________ leg is broken.**
5. **________________________ my favorite dessert.**
6. **________________________ the first door on the right.**
7. **________________________ petals are bright red.**
8. **The dog has eaten all of ________________________ food.**

Write a sentence of your own using *its*.

____

Write a sentence of your own using *it's*.

____

Name ______________________________ **Word Usage**

WHOSE AND WHO'S

Whose is a possessive pronoun and does not have an apostrophe.

Example: Whose book is that?

Who's is a contraction for *who is* or *who has* and has an apostrophe.

Example: Who's going to the fair? (Who is going to the fair?)
Who's eaten my cookie? (Who has eaten my cookie?)

Complete each sentence with *whose* or *who's*.

1. ______________________ **seen my lost pencil?**
2. ______________________ **pretty flowers are those?**
3. ______________________ **your favorite actor?**
4. ______________________ **bicycle is outside in the rain?**
5. ______________________ **on my baseball team?**
6. ______________________ **gloves are on the teacher's desk?**
7. ______________________ **dad can drive us to the hockey game?**
8. ______________________ **the kindest person you know?**

Write sentences about your family and friends with *whose* and *who's*.

1. **Who's** ____
2. **Whose** ____

Name ______________________________ Word Usage

YOUR AND YOU'RE

Your is a possessive pronoun and does not have an apostrophe.

Example: Your book is on the table.

You're is a contraction for *you are* and has an apostrophe.

Example: You're the best gardener I know.

Complete each sentence with *your* or *you're*.

1. **Is that ________________________ mom in the green van?**
2. **________________________ my closest friend.**
3. **________________________ speech was excellent!**
4. **Did you know that ________________________ first in line?**
5. **________________________ going to be late for the bus!**

Complete the paragraph using *your* or *you're*.

Is that ________________________ bicycle on the steps?

________________________ going to be in trouble for leaving it outside in the

rain. I bet ________________________ mom will be mad. What?

________________________ just washing it with rainwater?

________________________ car is getting washed too? Well, I hope

________________________ able to convince your mom that rainwater is

good for bicycles.

Name ________________________________ **Word Usage**

Knowing when to use *has* and *have* can be confusing. **Has** tells about one person, place or thing. **Have** is used with *I, you,* and with words that tell about more than one person, place, or thing.

Examples:

Drew has a computer.
The computer has a monitor.
I have a computer.
You have a printer.
The teachers have computers.

Write the correct word (*has* or *have*) to complete each sentence.

1. **Mrs. Peters ______________________ a collection of beautiful quilts.**
2. **The quilts ______________________ special places in her house.**
3. **Each quilt ______________________ its own colors and pattern.**
4. **One quilt ______________________ pink squares with flowers.**
5. **Mike Peters ______________________ a soccer quilt for his room.**
6. **Libby and Elena ______________________ new quilts for their beds.**
7. **The oldest quilt ______________________ hearts on it.**
8. **I don't ______________________ any quilts at my house.**

Write a sentence using the word *has*.

____

Write a sentence using the word *have*.

____

Name ______________________________ **Word Usage**

Knowing when to use *don't* and *doesn't* can be confusing. **Don't** is used with plural subjects and with the pronouns *I* and *you*. **Doesn't** is used with subjects that tell about one person, place, or thing.

Examples:

These flowers <u>don't</u> have a smell.
I <u>don't</u> know that song.
<u>Don't</u> these papers go in your folder?
<u>Doesn't</u> Margie like pizza?
My cat <u>doesn't</u> purr very often.
It <u>doesn't</u> take long to do my homework.

Write the correct word (*don't* or *doesn't*) to complete each sentence.

1. **Our toaster ______________________ work very well.**
2. **Some birds ______________________ fly south for the winter.**
3. **You ______________________ need to wake me up early tomorrow.**
4. **I sure ______________________ miss the cold weather!**
5. **That tree ______________________ have leaves; it has needles.**
6. **William ______________________ like to swim very much.**
7. **The computer ______________________ need a new monitor.**
8. **______________________ you like my new bicycle?**

Write a sentence using the word *don't*.

____

Write a sentence using the word *doesn't*.

____

Name ______________________________ **Word Usage**

GOOD OR WELL?

Good is an adjective and describes a noun or a pronoun.

Examples: That cake is really good. (*good* describes *cake*)
We had a good time at the beach. (*good* describes *time*)

Well is an adverb and describes a verb. Well can also be an adjective when it means "healthy."

Examples: Pam sang well. (How did Pam sing?)
Jerry feels well today. ("healthy")

Complete each sentence with *good* or *well*. Circle the word that good or well describes. The first one has been for you.

1. **Mark can play chess very ____well____.**
2. **The drums sound really ______________.**
3. **Our meeting went ______________.**
4. **Does Ashley dance as ______________ as Sarah?**
5. **You can get ______________ exercise with a jump rope.**
6. **The strawberries are ______________.**
7. **Can Tina sing ______________.**
8. **I had a ______________ time at the party yesterday.**
9. **The swimming pool feels ______________ in this hot weather.**
10. **Our class did ______________ on the spelling test.**

Name ______________________________ **Word Usage**

Words that are pronounced the same but have different spellings and different meanings are called **homonyms**.

Examples: The building is made of steel.
That robber plans to steal the diamonds.

Complete each sentence with the correct homonym.

1. **The party will be** ______________________________**.**
(hear / here)

   Can you ______________________________ **what I am saying?**
(hear / here)

2. **There were drops of** ______________________________ **on the grass.**
(dew / do)

   ______________________________ **you know what time it is?**
(dew / do)

3. **There are** ______________________________ **people in my family.**
(for / four)

   What are we having ______________________________ **supper?**
(for / four)

4. **I can** ______________________________ **far from this tower.**
(see / sea)

   We took our sailboat out on the ______________________________**.**
(see / sea)

5. **Our math test is next** ______________________________**.**
(week / weak)

   After running five miles I felt ______________________________**.**
(week / weak)

6. **I like** ______________________________ **spaghetti.**
(plane / plain)

   My cousin flies in his ______________________________**.**
(plane / plain)

Name ______________________________

Words that are pronounced the same but have different spellings and different meanings are called **homonyms**.

Examples: The wind blew my umbrella.
My favorite color is blue.

Complete each sentence with the correct homonym.

1. **May I have a ______________________ of cake?**
(peace / piece)

The war ended and ______________________ returned.
(peace / piece)

2. **There are ______________________ many bunnies in this cage.**
(two / to / too)

I have ______________________ pet bunnies.
(two / to / too)

I am going ______________________ the pet store.
(two / to / too)

3. **Your book is ______________________ the window.**
(buy / by / bye)

Will you ______________________ some milk at the store?
(buy / by / bye)

Please go tell Marie good ______________________.
(buy / by / bye)

4. **______________________ is a fly in my soup.**
(there / their)

Is this ______________________ cat?
(there / their)

5. **Ted dressed up as a ______________________.**
(knight / night)

Last ______________________ we went to the movies.
(knight / night)

6. **An octopus has ______________________ legs.**
(ate / eight)

Calvin ______________________ the last piece of pie.
(ate / eight)

Name ______________________________ **Word Usage**

A **negative** is a word that means "no". Here are some negative words: *no, not, none, never, no one, nothing* and the ending *-n't.* Use only ONE negative word in a sentence.

Examples:	Correct:	We never go to the skating rink.
	Incorrect:	We don't never go to the skating rink.
	Correct:	We never have anything to do.
	Incorrect:	We never have nothing to do.

Each sentence below has two negatives. Rewrite it correctly on the line. The first one has been done for you.

1. **Pam hasn't never gone to the movies.**

   Pam hasn't ever gone to the movies.

2. **We didn't see no bears in the forest.**

   ____

3. **Jim never had no problems with his homework.**

   ____

4. **The baker didn't have nothing left for me to buy.**

   ____

5. **Don't never leave the door open.**

   ____

6. **Joey doesn't have none of those toys.**

   ____

7. **My mom can't find no sugar for the cake.**

   ____

8. **I couldn't never lift that much weight!**

   ____

Name ______________________________

Remember to use **capital letters** when writing these things:

1. the first word in a sentence
2. the pronoun I
3. proper nouns—names of particular people, places, or things
4. important words in titles (of books, stories, movies, etc.)

Each sentence below has one or more capitalization mistakes. Write each sentence correctly on the line below it.

1. **The name of my school is fairmont elementary.**

   ____

2. **my favorite teacher is mrs. elgin.**

   ____

3. **My friend mary and i like our geography class best.**

   ____

4. **So far we have studied north america and europe.**

   ____

5. **Now we are studying brazil, a country in south america.**

   ____

6. **rio de janiero and sao paulo are two of brazil's big cities.**

   ____

7. **The amazon river flows through brazil.**

   ____

8. **i am reading a book called the amazon rainforest.**

   ____

Name ______________________________

Remember to use **capital letters** when writing these things:

1. the first word in a sentence
2. the pronoun *I*
3. proper nouns—names of particular people, places, or things
4. important words in titles (of books, stories, movies, etc.)

Each sentence below has one or more capitalization mistakes. Write each sentence correctly on the line below it.

1. **paris is the capital city of france.**

   ____

2. **The seine river flows through paris.**

   ____

3. **many people visit the eiffel tower.**

   ____

4. **Paris has a famous church called notre dame.**

   ____

5. **Another place to visit is the louvre, a famous art museum.**

   ____

6. **brigitte and jacques live in paris.**

   ____

7. **Their poodle fifi lives with them.**

   ____

8. **i would like to visit this city in france someday.**

   ____

Name ______________________________ **Titles**

The first word and all important words in a book title begin with a **capital letter**. Book titles are underlined when they are written.

Example: <u>Where the Red Fern Grows</u> is my favorite book.

Each sentence has a book title written in italics. Rewrite each book title with proper capitalization. Don't forget to underline the title!

1. **Last week I read *detective dan and the missing marble mystery*.**

   ____

2. **My little sister loves *read aloud bedtime stories*.**

   ____

3. ***charlotte's web* is a story about friendship.**

   ____

4. ***the word detective* is a funny book about nouns and verbs.**

   ____

5. **My mom just read a famous novel called *jane eyre*.**

   ____

6. **Dad always keeps *the world almanac* handy.**

   ____

Write the title of a book to answer each question.

1. **If you were to write a book, what would you title it?**

   ____

2. **Name one book that you would like to read.**

   ____

Name ________________________________ **Commas**

Commas (,) are used to separate words in a series (a list).

Example: Trees need sunlight, water, and carbon dioxide to make food.

Add commas where they are needed in the sentences below.

1. **Our air is composed of nitrogen oxygen and other gases.**
2. **Togas kimonos and saris are all types of clothing.**
3. **George Washington John Adams and Thomas Jefferson were the first three presidents of the United States.**
4. **Several parts of a knight's armor are the breastplate the helmet and the shield.**
5. **Yellowstone Badlands Glacier and Shenandoah are names of national parks.**
6. **Trumpets trombones and tubas are all brass instruments.**
7. **Louisa May Alcott wrote Little Women Little Men and Jo's Boys.**
8. **Science Spanish and American history are my favorite subjects to study.**

Write sentences using the words given in a series.

1. **red, yellow, and gold**

____

____

2. **rollerblades, skateboards, and bicycles**

____

____

Name ______________________________ **Commas**

Commas (,) are used to separate words in a series (a list).

Example: Grapefruit, oranges, tangerines, and lemons are citrus fruits.

Rewrite each sentence below using commas where they are needed.

1. **Sally bought some milk eggs and cheese at the store.**

   ____

   ____

2. **Please bring a pencil some paper and an eraser to school tomorrow.**

   ____

   ____

3. **When it's cold I wear my gloves scarf and hat.**

   ____

   ____

4. **Good sources of protein are meat fish eggs soybeans and nuts.**

   ____

   ____

5. **Each morning Peter wakes up takes a shower and eats breakfast.**

   ____

   ____

Name ______________________________ **Commas**

Commas are used to separate dates and years. Commas are used to separate cities and states.

Examples:	January 1, 1929	Baton Rouge, Louisiana
	April 15, 1975	Laramie, Wyoming

If the date or address is in the middle of a sentence, a comma also follows the year and the state.

Examples: On October 12, 1492, Columbus reached land.
We visited Jackson, Mississippi, on our vacation.

Put commas where they belong in the dates and places below.

March 23 1995	**Blacksburg Virginia**
May 8 1967	**Chicago Illinois**
August 5 1876	**Fargo North Dakota**
September 13 1996	**Atlanta Georgia**
December 25 1913	**Needles California**

Correct these sentences by putting commas where they are needed for dates and places.

1. **On July 4 1776 the Declaration of Independence was accepted.**
2. **We visited Philadelphia Pennsylvania and Baltimore Maryland.**
3. **On March 12 1996 our state will have an election.**
4. **We just moved from Canyonville Oregon to Norwood Massachusetts.**
5. **Did you know that on May 11 1858 Minnesota became a state?**
6. **Enid Oklahoma is a fine city to visit.**

Name ______________________________ **Contractions**

A **contraction** is two words that are put together to make one shorter word. One kind of contraction is made with a verb + not. An apostrophe is used in a contraction to show where letters have been left out.

Examples:

can + not = can't	do + not = don't
is + not = isn't	are + not = aren't
have + not = haven't	was + not = wasn't
will + not = won't	

Write each sentence on the line, changing the underlined words to a contraction.

1. **I can not play ball this afternoon.**

   ____

2. **It just is not possible.**

   ____

3. **I do not have the time.**

   ____

4. **I will not be able to play until my book report is done.**

   ____

Write a sentence using each contraction.

1. **can't**

   ____

2. **aren't**

   ____

3. **don't**

   ____

Name ______________________________ **Contractions**

A **contraction** is two words that are put together to make one shorter word. One kind of contraction is made with a pronoun + a verb. An apostrophe is used in a contraction to show where letters have been left out.

Examples:	I + am = I'm	you + will = you'll
	he + will = he'll	we + are = we're
	it + is = it's	they + are = they're
	I + would = I'd	I + have = I've

Match the words on the left with the contractions on the right.

1. ________ We are	**A) He'd**
2. ________ I will	**B) I'll**
3. ________ She is	**C) There's**
4. ________ There is	**D) We're**
5. ________ He would	**E) She's**

Complete the story by adding contractions made from the words below each line.

________________ (We are) **taking my dad to the airport today.** ________________ (He is) **going on a business trip to Washington, D.C., but** ________________ (he will) **be back on Thursday.** ________________ (I am) **always happy to go to the airport.** ________________ (It is) **such an exciting place! I hope** ________________ (I will) **get to see some fighter jets.** ________________ (They are) **amazing.** ________________ (I have) **always wanted to ride in one.**

Name ______________________________ **Quotes**

Quotation marks (" ") are used when writing a person's exact words.

1. Put quotation marks before and after a person's words.
2. Use a comma, question mark, or exclamation point to separate the spoken words from the rest of the sentence.
3. Begin the quote (the spoken words) with a capital letter.

Examples: "We should get an animal," I said.
"Would you really like a pet?" said Mom.
"Let's get a cat!" yelled my sister.

Add quotation marks where they belong in the sentences below.

1. I think a dog would make a good pet, I said.

2. Dogs are loyal and smart, replied Mom.

3. Then she asked, What kind of dog would you like?

4. Let me think about it, I answered.

Rewrite each sentence adding quotation marks and punctuation.

1. I found a book about dogs in the library I told Mom.

____

2. I think a spaniel would be a good pet I said.

____

3. But how big do they get she asked.

____

4. They are medium-sized I replied.

____

5. Let's start looking for a spaniel declared Mom.

____

Name ______________________________ Quotes

Quotation marks (“ ”) are used when writing a person’s exact words.

1. Put quotation marks before and after a person’s words.
2. Use a comma, question mark, or exclamation point to separate the spoken words from the rest of the sentence.
3. Begin the quote (the spoken words) with a capital letter.

Examples: “How was your vacation?” asked Ben.
“I had a great time,” replied Kyle.

Add quotation marks and punctuation marks to the sentences below.

1. I just went to the moon declared Kyle.

2. No way stated Ben.

3. Well, I went to a place like the moon said Kyle.

4. It’s called Craters of the Moon National Monument he added.

5. It’s in Idaho and we stopped there on our vacation said Kyle.

6. Why is it called Craters of the Moon asked Ben.

7. Lava from a volcano hardened into rock Kyle said.

8. All you can see for miles around is bare rock covering the ground. It looks just like the moon.

9. Ben laughed and said Maybe I’ll go to the moon someday, too!

10. Until you do you can look at my pictures and pretend with me said Kyle.

Write your own quote with quotation marks to answer the question.

What would you say if you really landed on the moon?

____

____

Name ______________________________ **Proofreading**

Reading over your work to check it is called **proofreading**. Proofreading is important at school and also at home (like when you write a letter to a relative or friend). When you proofread something you have written, check spelling, capital letters, punctuation marks, and grammar (to see that you have used words correctly).

Examples:

BEFORE PROOFREADING	AFTER PROOFREADING
Did Tom name his puppy maverick.	Did Tom name his puppy **Maverick**?
We was going to the movies.	We **were** going to the movies.
"Please pass the peas, I said.	"Please pass the peas," I said.

Proofread each sentence below and draw a circle around the error or where something is missing. Write the sentence correctly on the line. (The number after the sentence tells how many mistakes can be found.)

1. **kenya is a country in eastern africa. (2)**

   ____

2. **The indian ocean lies on the southeast coast of Kenya. (2)**

   ____

3. **Does Kenya really have many wild cheetahs and lions. (1)**

   ____

4. **Mt. elgon National Park is a good plac to see elephants. (2)**

   ____

5. **Many visitors goes exploring in Kenyas wildlife parks. (2)**

   ____

6. **the bigest city in Kenya is nairobi. (3)**

   ____

7. **Nairobi are also the capital city (2)**

   ____

Name ______________________________

Reading over your work to check it is called **proofreading**. Proofreading is important at school and also at home (like when you write a letter to a relative or friend). When you proofread something you have written, check spelling, capital letters, punctuation marks, and grammar (to see that you have used words correctly).

Examples:

BEFORE PROOFREADING	AFTER PROOFREADING
Im leaving for schol.	**I'm** leaving for **school**.
I has no money for lunch.	I **have** no money for lunch.
In May 1989 I was born.	In May**,** 1989**,** I was born.

Dan wrote the paragraph below for social studies, but he forgot to proofread it! Read Dan's paragraph and draw a circle where something is incorrect or missing. Then rewrite the paragraph correctly below. There are 20 mistakes.

PIKE DISCOVERS A MOUNTAIN

Zebulon pike were an explorer who helped people learn more about north america In 1806 he left St. Louis missouri and headed west? He traveled up the arkansas river to the rocky mountains. In novermber 1906 he find a huge muntain. The mountain was named Pike s Peak and is now the most famous mountain in colorado. this discovery and Pike's other travels gave people important information about the southwestern part of Narth America.

____

____

____

____

____

____

____

Name ______________________________ Proofreading

Bill has just written a fan letter. He forgot to proofread it. Find 20 mistakes in the letter. Then rewrite the letter correctly on the lines below.

March 9 1999

dear mr Hoops,

my mane is Bill and i am your biggest fan. i love basketball and I really lov waching you play You is a great basketball player. Do you practice every day.

i herd that you use some of your money to hep kids go to college. You must be a really nise guy, too. could you please sent me a picture.

Your friend,

Bill

Answer Key

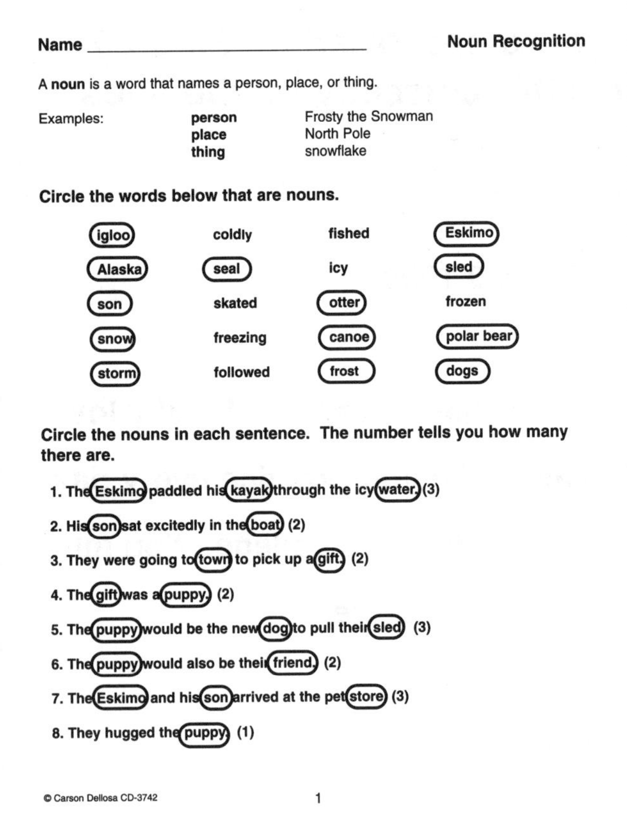

Name ______________________ **Noun Recognition**

A **noun** is a word that names a person, place, or thing.

Examples:	**person**	Frosty the Snowman
	place	North Pole
	thing	snowflake

Circle the words below that are nouns.

igloo	coldly	fished	Eskimo
Alaska	seal	icy	sled
son	skated	otter	frozen
snow	freezing	canoe	polar bear
storm	followed	frost	dogs

Circle the nouns in each sentence. The number tells you how many there are.

1. The Eskimo paddled his kayak through the icy water. (3)
2. His son sat excitedly in the boat. (2)
3. They were going to town to pick up a gift. (2)
4. The gift was a puppy. (2)
5. The puppy would be the new dog to pull their sled. (3)
6. The puppy would also be their friend. (2)
7. The Eskimo and his son arrived at the pet store. (3)
8. They hugged the puppy. (1)

Name ______________________ **Noun Recognition**

A **noun** is a word that names a person, place, or thing.

Example: Ranger Rick park moose

Read the nouns below and write them in the correct columns.

Dr. Doolittle	Adams Park	tree
shoe	New York	Mr. Ranger
Mr. Canyon	Karen's Café	Buffalo Bill
wildflower	box	Western Inn
picnic	Harry	Ohio

Person	Place	Thing
Dr. Doolittle	Adams Park	shoe
Mr. Canyon	New York	wild flower
Harry	Karen's Café	picnic
Mr. Ranger	Western Inn	box
Buffalo Bill	Ohio	tree

Circle the nouns in each sentence. The number tells you how many there are.

1. My family visited Yellowstone National Park (2)
2. Yellowstone has amazing sites (2)
3. We saw moose elk and buffalo (3)
4. There are geysers where hot water and steam shoot out of the ground. (4)

Name ______________________ **Common Nouns**

A **common noun** names any person, place, or thing.

Examples:	Common Nouns	Not Common Nouns
	store	Joe's Market
	uncle	Uncle Bruce
	dog	Snoopy

Circle the common noun in each pair of words below.

1. cow	Bessie	6. book	*Ted the Toad*
2. park	Lincoln Park	7. Christmas	holiday
3. Rouge River	river	8. May	month
4. doctor	Doctor Baker	9. girl	Sarah
5. Chicago	city	10. day	Monday

Circle the common noun in each sentence.

1. My cat is named Frisky.
2. Julie is my cousin.
3. My favorite drink is Kool Kola.
4. We eat turkey on Thanksgiving Day.
5. On Monday I go to school.
6. Iceland is a country I want to visit.
7. My house is on Main Street.
8. Her name is Rose
9. My favorite holiday is Valentine's Day.
10. Is your cat's name Fluffy?

Name ______________________ **Common Nouns**

A **common noun** names any person, place, or thing.

Examples:	Common Nouns	Not Common Nouns
	boat	Titanic
	ocean	Pacific Ocean
	sailor	Captain Cook

Circle the common nouns in each sentence. The number tells you how many there are.

1. Boats are used all over the world. (2)
2. The first boats were developed from rafts. (2)
3. Ancient Egyptians were the first people to add sails to boats. (3)
4. Native Americans and early settlers used canoes. (2)
5. A canoe is a long, thin boat moved by paddles. (3)
6. A ship is a large boat made to travel on oceans. (3)
7. Ships carry passengers and freight and are used to fight battles. (4)
8. Two famous ships are the Mayflower and the Santa Maria. (1)

Read the clues and write the common noun they describe.

mug 1. I hold coffee and you drink from me.

telephone 2. You use me to call people. I have push buttons and you hold me to your ear.

computer 3. I have a keyboard and a monitor. Many people use me when they write and work.

dog 4. I am a furry pet that barks.

Answer Key

Name ______________________ **Proper Nouns**

A **proper noun** names a specific person, place, or thing.

Examples: George Washington, White House, Virginia, Rover

Days of the week, months of the year, holidays, and book titles are also proper nouns.

Examples: Monday, June, Valentine's Day, *United States History*

Read the nouns listed below. Write the proper nouns in the blanks.

Mount Vernon	**president**	**Martha Washington**
general	**February**	**Revolutionary War**
Presidents' Day	**state**	**colony**
horse	**leader**	**General Washington**
Mrs. Brown	**paper**	**December**

Proper Nouns

Mount Vernon	Martha Washington
Presidents' Day	Revolutionary War
Mrs. Brown	General Washington
February	December

Circle the proper nouns in each sentence.

1. **George Washington lived in the state of Virginia.**
2. **George Washington first proved himself a leader when he was a general.**
3. **He led the American Colonies to victory during the Revolutionary War.**
4. **He was then elected to be the first president of the United States.**
5. **He and his wife, Martha, lived in a home known as Mount Vernon.**

© Carson Dellosa CD-3742 5

Name ______________________ **Proper Nouns**

A **proper noun** names a specific person, place, or thing and is always capitalized.

Examples: Harold Hill, Krispy Krinkles, Lake Michigan, Lassie

Days of the week, months of the year, holidays, and book titles are also proper nouns.

Examples: Tuesday, March, Mother's Day, *Max and the Mud Pie Mystery*

Fill in each blank with a proper noun.

1. **A holiday I like is** Christmas.
2. **One of my relatives is named** Bob.
3. **The last book I read was** The Old Man and the Sea.
4. **One of the summer months is** July.
5. **The day of the week today is** Sunday.
6. **The state where I was born is** Louisiana.
7. **The day of the week yesterday was** Saturday.
8. **A restaurant I like is called** Robert's Reef.
9. **My favorite month is** April.
10. **My mother's name is** Kay.

Write the proper noun from each sentence in the blank.

Inspector 1. **My dog's name is Inspector.**

Candy 2. **Mary had her cat, Candy, with her.**

Canada 3. **Last week I went to Canada.**

© Carson Dellosa CD-3742 6

Name ______________________ **Common & Proper Noun Review**

Common nouns name any one of a group of persons, places, or things.
Proper nouns name a specific person, place, or thing.

Write each noun below in the column where it belongs.

state	**Uncle Joe**	**President Truman**
Japan	**Tweety**	**planet**
forest	**Yosemite Park**	**cousin**
dollar	**orange**	**Mayflower**

Common Nouns	Proper Nouns
state	Japan
forest	Uncle Joe
dollar	Tweety
orange juice	Yosemite Park
planet	President Truman
cousin	Mayflower

Read the paragraph below. Circle the common nouns (14) and underline the proper nouns (14).

A Famous Monument

The Black Hills of South Dakota are home to a towering and majestic monument. The monument, called Mount Rushmore, is a beautiful carving on the side of a mountain. The carving is of four great presidents: George Washington, Thomas Jefferson, Abraham Lincoln, and Teddy Roosevelt. Mount Rushmore was carved by a sculptor named Gutzon Borglum. Borglum and his crew spent fourteen years carving Mount Rushmore. Today it stands as a symbol of the United States. A trip to the state of South Dakota is not complete without a visit to Mount Rushmore.

© Carson Dellosa CD-3742 7

Name ______________________ **Common & Proper Noun Review**

Common nouns name any one of a group of persons, places, or things.
Proper nouns name a specific person, place, or thing.

Each sentence has one common noun and one proper noun. Write the common noun to the left of the sentence and the proper noun to the right.

Common Nouns		Proper Nouns
song	**My favorite song is Edelweiss.**	*Edelweiss*
bear	**Smokey is a famous bear.**	Smokey
family	**My family ate at Pizza Barn.**	Pizza Barn
city	**Ogden is a beautiful city.**	Ogden
scientist	**Isaac Newton was a scientist.**	Isaac Newton
satellite	**The first satellite was Sputnik I.**	Sputnik I
cameras	**George Eastman made cameras.**	George Eastman
months	**The Pilgrims sailed for two months.**	Pilgrims
poet	**Emily Dickinson was a poet.**	Emily Dickinson

Write a common noun AND a proper noun for each category.

	Common	Proper
1. a place to visit	park	Central Park
2. a place to play	back yard	Dimple's Fun House
3. a neighbor	girl	Judy

© Carson Dellosa CD-3742 8

Answer Key

Name ____________________ **Common & Proper Noun Review**

Circle all proper nouns in the sentences below. Underline all the common nouns. (The first number after the sentence tells how many proper nouns are in the sentence. The second number tells how many common nouns there are.)

1. The (Pony Express) was the first direct-mail service to the western territories of (North America.) (2, 2)
2. The (Pony Express) started in (St. Joseph, Missouri) and ended in (Sacramento, California) (3, 0)
3. The (Pony Express) was started in (January, 1860,) by a company named (Russell, Majors, and Waddell) (3, 1)
4. This service delivered mail from (Missouri) to (California) in ten days! (2, 3)
5. Riders passed through eight states, crossing rivers, plains, and the (Rocky Mountains) as they rode to the west coast. (1, 5)
6. The first rider left (Missouri) on (April 3, 1860.) (2, 1)
7. He arrived in (Sacramento) in nine days and 23 hours. (1, 2)
8. The first mail included a letter from (President Buchanan) to the governor of (California.) (2, 3)
9. The most famous rider for the (Pony Express) was (William F. Cody,) also known as (Buffalo Bill.) (3, 1)
10. The (Pony Express) was helpful, but it only lasted 18 months. (1, 1)
11. The telegraph had been invented by (Samuel Morse.) (1, 1)
12. A telegraph line was built across (North America.) (1, 1)
13. Messages were sent to (California) more quickly and safely by this telegraph. (1, 2)
14. The telegraph put an end to the (Pony Express.) (1, 2)

© Carson-Dellosa CD-3742 9

Name ____________________ **Plural Nouns**

A **plural noun** names more than one person, place, or thing. Most nouns are made plural by adding **-s**.

Examples: friends islands hamburgers

To make nouns ending in *-x*, *-s*, *-ch*, and *-sh* plural, add **-es**.

Examples: foxes guesses benches wishes

Write the plural for each noun.

hunch hunches reflex reflexes
kangaroo kangaroos miss misses
porch porches machine machines

Write the correct plural noun to complete each sentence.

1. One of my birthday wishes (wish) came true!
2. I wished for a trip to City Island with my friends (friend).
3. We did many wonderful things (thing) on City Island.
4. We sat on benches (bench) and ate ice cream.
5. We played three rounds (round) of Water Golf.
6. We bought kites (kite) and flew them.
7. Then we ate our lunches (lunch) by the river.
8. I wish there were more days (day) like this.

© Carson-Dellosa CD-3742 10

Name ____________________ **Plural Nouns**

A **plural noun** names more than one person, place, or thing. Most nouns are made plural by adding **-s**.

Examples: bakers gardens grapes

To make nouns ending in *-x*, *-s*, *-ch*, and *-sh* plural, add **-es**.

Examples: taxes glasses churches bushes

Complete the story below by adding the correct plural nouns.

I like many kinds (kind) of fruits, but my mom knows that my favorite is peaches (peach). One of my favorite foods (food) in the world is a juicy, peach pie. Mom doesn't make pies (pie) very often, though. Yesterday, she ran errands (errand) and came back with something special for me. She gave me three guesses (guess) to find out what it was. My first guess was some socks (sock). My second guess was bunches (bunch) of grapes. My third guess was some pencils (pencil). Then mom showed me two boxes (box) of peaches (peach). "My favorite," I yelled as I gave mom two kisses (kiss). "Peach pie for dessert," mom said and smiled.

© Carson-Dellosa CD-3742 11

Name ____________________ **Plural Nouns**

A **plural noun** names more than one person, place, or thing.

To form the plural of a noun that ends with a consonant then **y**, change the **-y** to **-i** and add **-es**.

Examples: I rode a pony at the fair. Jim rode two ponies.

If the noun ends in a vowel then **y**, just add **-s**.

Examples: Dad lost his car key. Dad lost all his keys.

Write the plural form of each noun.

city cities toy toys
cry cries story stories
baby babies tray trays

Write the correct plural nouns to complete each sentence.

1. There are two libraries (library) in our town.
2. Two ladies (lady) work in the library by my house.
3. There are also two bakeries (bakery) in town.
4. They sell tarts with cherries (cherry) for pennies (penny).
5. Our town's pet store has guppies (guppy), puppies (puppy), and monkeys (monkey)!

© Carson-Dellosa CD-3742 12

Answer Key

Name ______________________ **Plural Nouns**

A **plural noun** names more than one person, place, or thing.

To form the plural of a noun that ends with a consonant then **-y**, change the **-y** to **-i** and add **-es**.

Examples: I live in a city. I have lived in three different cities.

If the noun ends in a vowel then -y, just add **-s**.

Examples: Our house has a chimney. Our last house had two chimneys.

Complete the sentences by adding the correct plural nouns.

Aunt Nancy's home is surrounded by hills and valleys (valley). **Wild** berries (berry) **grow in the valleys. When our** families (family) **got together this year, Aunt Nancy took all the children berry picking. All my cousins, both the** boys (boy) **and the girls, loved picking** berries (berry). **They tasted so good! We even found fruit trees with wild** cherries (cherry). **A large family of white** bunnies (bunny) **was playing in some** lilies (lily). **I hope we can stay with Aunt Nancy for many** days (day) **next year and pick** berries (berry) **in the** valleys (valley) **again.**

Name ______________________ **Plural Nouns**

A **plural noun** names more than one person, place, or thing. The plural of some nouns is formed with a brand new word. A few words are spelled the same whether they mean one or more than one.

Examples: Ted lost a tooth. Tracy lost two teeth.
Bambi is a deer. All the deer liked salt.

Match each noun on the left with its plural form on the right.

E	**woman**	**A. feet**
D	**sheep**	**B. children**
B	**child**	**C. oxen**
F	**moose**	**D. sheep**
A	**foot**	**E. women**
C	**ox**	**F. moose**

Complete each sentence with the plural form of the given noun. Use a dictionary if you are not sure.

1. **The trumpet players in the band were all** men (man).
2. **My sister likes to feed the** geese (goose) **at the park.**
3. **We saw three white** sheep (sheep) **and one black sheep.**
4. **My family has two grown-ups and two** children (child).
5. **Tabby, our cat, caught five** mice (mouse) **last night.**

Name ______________________ **Plural Noun Review**

Write the plural form of each noun.

fox foxes	**kite** kites	**boy** boys
city cities	**tooth** teeth	**reflex** reflexes
deer deer	**child** children	**party** parties
box boxes	**brush** brushes	**bus** buses
valley valleys	**church** churches	**paint** paints

Write the plural form of the missing nouns to complete the paragraph. Use a dictionary if you are not sure.

Life for cowboys (cowboy) **is exciting, but it is also hard work. Most cowboys work on big** ranches (ranch), **taking care of all the** horses (horse) **and** cows (cow). **It is the cowboy's job to feed the** animals (animal) **and to make sure they stay healthy. Each year when** calves (calf) **are born, the cowboys brand them and give them** shots (shot). **If a calf gets sick, then he gives the calf medicine** drops (drop). **Cowboys also put new** shoes (shoe) **on horses and check their** teeth (tooth) **to learn how old they are. They even mend** fences (fence).

Name ______________________ **Compound Nouns**

Words that are made up of two smaller words are called **compound words**.

Examples: lighthouse, fireplace, classroom, cookbook, newspaper, chalkboard

Match the words on the left with the words on the right to make compound words. Then write the words on the lines.

play	**crow**	1. playmate
meat	**toes**	2. meatloaf
sun	**boat**	3. sunset
scare	**mate**	4. scarecrow
sail	**set**	5. sailboat
tip	**loaf**	6. tiptoes

Write the compound word that completes each sentence.

1. **A fish shaped like a star is a** starfish
2. **An ache in your head is a** headache
3. **A room for a bed is a** bedroom
4. **The shore along the sea is the** seashore
5. **Light given by candles is** candlelight
6. **A man who delivers mail is a** mailman
7. **A box for shoes is a** shoe box

Answer Key

Name ______________________________ **Possessive Nouns**

A **possessive noun** shows who or what is the owner of something. To make a singular noun possessive add an apostrophe before the **s**.

Example: Kevin's basketball went through the hoop.

To make a plural noun possessive, add an apostrophe after the **s**.

Example: The other boys' balls just hit the rim.

Write the noun in each sentence so that it shows possession. (Some are singular and some are plural.)

1. The basketball ___team's___ (team) coach is Mr. Dribble.
2. ___Mr. Dribble's___ (Mr. Dribble) first name is Dan.
3. ___Dan's___ (Dan) favorite night is Friday.
4. Every Friday the ___school's___ (school) gym is full of fans.
5. ___Parent's___ (Parents) cheers can be heard in the stands.
6. ___Cheerleader's___ (Cheerleaders) pompons wave in the air.
7. The ___player's___ (players) families cheer as the team wins.
8. The ___team's___ (team) mascot does a cartwheel.
9. The ___school's___ (school) bus takes everyone to the ice cream shop.
10. The ___bus's___ (bus) driver is named Mr. Ed.

Name ______________________________ **Possessive Nouns**

A **possessive noun** shows who or what is the owner of something. To make a singular noun possessive add an apostrophe before the **s**.

Example: The jewelry box's diamonds were gone!

To make a plural noun possessive, add an apostrophe after the **s**.

Example: Police cars' sirens were heard everywhere.

Write each noun in the sentence so that it shows possession. Underline the thing that belongs or is owned by the noun. The first one has been done for you.

1. The ___*judge's*___ (judge) gavel hit the bench and the trial began.
2. The ___courtroom's___ (courtroom) noise stopped.
3. One lawyer told the jury what happened to ___Mrs. Ruby's___ (Mrs. Ruby) diamonds.
4. The ___lawyer's___ (lawyer) speech went on for many hours.
5. By the end of the day, the ___jewelry's___ (jewelry) whereabouts was still unclear.
6. Finally the ___judge's___ (judge) voice was heard.
7. "Does your speech have anything to do with the ___diamonds'___ (diamonds) disappearance?" he asked.
8. "You are testing the ___court's___ (court) patience!"
9. Suddenly a ___police officer's___ (police officer) footsteps were heard.
10. "I found the missing jewels in ___Mrs. Ruby's___ (Mrs. Ruby) trunk!" he announced.

Name ______________________________ **Subject Pronouns**

A **pronoun** is a word that can take the place of a noun. *I, you, he, she, it, we,* and *they* are **subject pronouns**.

Examples: **Abraham Lincoln** was the 16th president.
He was the 16th president.

Betty loves art class
She loves art class

Change each sentence by using a pronoun in place of the underlined words.

1. My friends are coming over today.
   ___They___ are coming over today.
2. Frank and I love to go to the movies.
   ___We___ love to go to the movies.
3. Maria is the best speller in our class.
   ___She___ is the best speller in our class.
4. Jonathon reads a new book each week.
   ___He___ reads a new book each week.
5. That flower has beautiful colors.
   ___It___ has beautiful colors.
6. My mom and dad are going out to dinner.
   ___They___ are going out to dinner.

Name ______________________________ **Subject Pronouns**

A **pronoun** is a word that can take the place of a noun. *I, you, he, she, it, we,* and *they* are **subject pronouns**.

Examples: **Dad** works at a television station.
He works at a television station.

The station is an exciting place to work.
It is an exciting place to work.

Change each sentence by using a pronoun in place of the underlined words.

1. My family just took my sister to college.
   ___They___ just took my sister to college.
2. My sister finished high school last year.
   ___She___ finished high school last year.
3. Now Sis wants to study to be a journalist.
   Now ___she___ wants to study to be a journalist.
4. Mom and Dad helped Sis get ready for college.
   ___They___ helped Sis get ready for college.
5. A scholarship will help Sis to pay for her studies.
   ___It___ will help Sis to pay for her studies.
6. Yesterday Sis and I got to see the dorm where she will live.
   Yesterday ___we___ got to see the dorm where she will live.
7. The room was small, but cozy.
   ___It___ was small, but cozy.

Answer Key

Name ______________________ **Object Pronouns**

A **pronoun** is a word that can take the place of a noun. *Me, him, her, it, us, you,* and *them* are **object pronouns**.

Examples: Vince threw **the ball**. — Vince threw **it**.
The dog licked **Kim**. — The dog licked **her**.

Change each sentence by using a pronoun in place of the underlined words.

1. Gary got a camera for Christmas.

   Gary got ___it___ for Christmas.
2. He took a whole roll of pictures in one day.

   He took a whole roll of ___them___ in one day.
3. One picture showed Mom cooking pancakes.

   One picture showed ___her___ cooking pancakes.
4. Then he took a picture of Lucy and me.

   Then he took a picture of ___us___.
5. Gary took the film to be developed the next day.

   Gary took ___it___ to be developed the next day.

Write a sentence for each of the pronouns given.

1. him I gave the book to him.
2. them Can we go with them?
3. me That belongs to me.
4. us Please sit by us.

Name ______________________ **Object Pronouns**

A **pronoun** is a word that can take the place of a noun. *Me, him, her, it, us, you,* and *them* are **object pronouns**.

Examples: Peggy helped **Jake**. — Peggy helped **him**.
We ate **pretzels**. — We ate **them**.
Peggy phoned **Toni and Mac**. — Peggy phoned **them**.

Change each sentence by using a pronoun in place of the underlined words.

1. Peggy called Toni yesterday.

   Peggy called ___her___ yesterday.
2. Peggy invited Toni and her brother to go swimming in her pool.

   Peggy invited ___them___ to go swimming in her pool.
3. Toni threw the phone down.

   Toni threw ___it___ down.
4. She and her brother put their bathing suits on quickly.

   She and her brother put ___them___ on quickly.
5. Their mom drove the car to Peggy's house.

   Their mom drove ___it___ to Peggy's house.
6. The kids played water games all day.

   The kids played ___them___ all day.
7. Toni and Peggy taught Toni's brother how to dive.

   Toni and Peggy taught ___him___ how to dive.
8. "Peggy is so nice to share this pool with us," said Toni.

   Peggy is so nice to share ___it___ with us.

Name ______________________ **Possessive Pronouns**

These **possessive pronouns** come right before nouns and show ownership: *my, his, her, its, our, your,* and *their.*

Example: Abigail's room is pink. — Her room is pink.

These **possessive pronouns** are used alone: *mine, his, hers, its, ours, yours,* and *theirs.*

Example: That is Abigail's stuffed bear. — That is hers.

Replace the underlined word in each sentence with the correct possessive pronoun.

1. Toady is the family's frog.

   Toady is ___their___ frog.
2. Toady's collar is red.

   ___His___ collar is red.
3. The collar's inscription says "123 Hickory Street."

   ___Its___ inscription says "123 Hickory Street."
4. That big fish tank is Toady's home.

   That big fish tank is ___his___ home.
5. Sometimes Toady eats the fishs' food.

   Sometimes Toady eats ___their___ food.

Rewrite each sentence replacing the underlined words with a possessive pronoun.

1. That frog is our frog. That frog is ours.
2. This frog is my frog. This frog is mine.

Name ______________________ **Possessive Pronouns**

These **possessive pronouns** come right before nouns and show ownership: *my, his, her, its, our, your,* and *their.*

Example: **The player's uniforms** are blue. — **Their** uniforms are blue.

These **possessive pronouns** are used alone: *mine, his, hers, its, ours, yours,* and *theirs.*

Example: That is **Harry's uniform**. — That is **his**.

Replace the underlined word in each sentence with the correct possessive pronoun.

1. The Pilgrims' ship was called the Mayflower.

   ___Their___ ship was called the Mayflower.
2. Christopher Columbus' biggest ship was the Santa Maria.

   ___His___ biggest ship was the Santa Maria.
3. Penelope is the nickname of my grandma's car.

   Penelope is the nickname of ___her___ car.
4. My toy airplane's name is King of the Sky.

   ___Its___ name is King of the Sky.
5. The *Spirit of St. Louis* was the name of Charles Lindbergh's airplane.

   The *Spirit of St. Louis* was the name of ___his___ airplane.

Rewrite each sentence replacing the underlined pronouns with a possessive pronouns.

1. That rocket is Tony's. That rocket is his.
2. That is the astronaut's rocket. That is his rocket.

Answer Key

Name ______________________ **Recognizing Verbs**

Verbs are action words. They tell what a person or thing is doing.

Examples: My mom **sews** pretty clothes. Dad **builds** furniture.

Circle the verb in each sentence.

1. **Kimberly's class gave a talent show.**
2. **Ricky played his tuba.**
3. **Connie sang her favorite song.**
4. **Derrick told jokes.**
5. **David and Donald did magic tricks.**
6. **Sandy danced the Cha-cha.**

Complete each sentence with a verb from the word bank.

1. **A talent is something you naturally** ___do___ **well.**
2. **Everyone** ___has___ **talents.**
3. **Some people** ___draw___ **and paint beautiful pictures.**
4. **Others** ___play___ **sports and games well.**
5. **Some people** ___sing___ **with beautiful voices.**
6. **Chefs** ___use___ **their talent to cook nice meals.**

WORD BANK

use play has know sing do draw

Name ______________________ **Recognizing Verbs**

Verbs are action words. They tell what a person or thing is doing.

Examples: Mike **exercises** every day. He **eats** healthy foods. Our eyes **help** us to see. Our bones **give** our bodies shape.

Circle the verb in each sentence.

1. **Your body works hard every minute of the day.**
2. **Your heart pumps blood with oxygen and nutrients to your cells.**
3. **Lungs filter oxygen from the air.**
4. **Your stomach breaks down food into smaller parts.**
5. **Muscles and joints work together to help you move.**
6. **Your brain controls your body's work.**

Complete each sentence with a verb from the word bank.

1. **Skin is a covering that** ___protects___ **our bodies.**
2. **Skin** ___keeps___ **out dirt and germs.**
3. **Nerves in your skin help you** ___feel___ **things like pain or cold.**
4. **When our bodies are too hot, we** ___sweat___ **from openings in our skin.**
5. **Our bodies** ___cool___ **down when the sweat evaporates.**

WORD BANK

sweat wear protects feel cool hurts keeps

Name ______________________ **Linking Verbs**

The verb **to be** is a special kind of verb called a **linking verb**. Instead of showing action, **to be** links the subject of the sentence to the rest of the sentence and tells us something about or describes the subject. Here are some forms of **to be** in the present tense:

Singular	Plural
(I) am	(we) are
(you) are	(you) are
(He, she, it) is	(they) are

Examples: I am in the fourth grade. Chicago is a big city. My parents are smart.

Complete each sentence with the correct form of the verb to be.

1. **A group of baby kittens** ___is___ **a litter.**
2. **Kittens** ___are___ **blind and helpless when they are born.**
3. **The mother cat** ___is___ **aware that her kittens need help.**
4. **She** ___is___ **gentle as she cares for them.**
5. **Kittens** ___are___ **ready to open their eyes in 10-14 days.**
6. **They** ___are___ **able to see especially well at night.**
7. **Kittens** ___are___ **also good at balancing and can move quickly.**
8. **I** ___am___ **so glad that I have a kitten!**

Name ______________________ **Linking Verbs**

The verb **to be** is a special kind of verb called a **linking verb**. Instead of showing action, **to be** links the subject of the sentence to the rest of the sentence and tells us something about or describes the subject. Here are some forms of **to be** in the present tense:

Singular	Plural
(I) was	(we) were
(you) were	(you) were
(he, she, it) was	(they) were

Examples: I was on vacation last week. My dad was our tour guide. Mom and Sis were our map readers.

Complete the sentences with past tense forms of to be.

1. **The coast of Oregon** ___was___ **a great place to visit.**
2. **The mountain cliffs** ___were___ **amazing.**
3. **The beach** ___was___ **covered with sand and shells.**
4. **Baby seals** ___were___ **out on the sand bars with their mothers.**
5. **Tide pools** ___were___ **filled with starfish and sea urchins.**
6. **In the distance, a whale** ___was___ **swimming in the ocean.**
7. **The ocean** ___was___ **too cold to swim in, but we didn't care.**
8. **We really** ___were___ **sad when it was time to leave the Oregon coast.**

Answer Key

Name ______________________ **Helping Verbs**

Helping verbs are sometimes used with action verbs. Here is a list of common helping verbs:

am	were	shall	should	must
is	has	will	would	do
are	have	can	could	did
was	had	may	might	does

Examples: I am going on a trip. We might see a moose.

Use a helping verb from the word bank to complete each sentence.

1. The Browns were getting ready for their vacation.
2. "We should take our coats," said Mrs. Brown.
3. "It will be cold in the mountains."
4. Scott was excited.
5. Mr. Brown had said he wants to take us hiking.
6. "We might see some bears in the mountains!" exclaimed little Amy.
7. "We can look for animals," replied mom.
8. "I am hoping that we see some."
9. "We must come here again soon!" said Mr. Brown.

WORD BANK

will	were	would	had	am
should	was	can	might	must

© Carson Dellosa CD-3742 29

Name ______________________ **Helping Verbs**

Helping verbs are sometimes used with action verbs. Here is a list of common helping verbs:

am	were	shall	should	must
is	has	will	would	do
are	have	can	could	did
was	had	may	might	does

Examples: It has snowed all night. School will be canceled.

Complete each sentence with a helping verb from the list above. Some sentences may have more than one correct answer.

1. I shall eat broccoli for dinner.
2. I am going to ask for corn tomorrow.
3. I think Mom might cook macaroni and cheese too.
4. Dad is like that.
5. The best dinner would be pizza and ice cream.

Use the verb pairs listed to write your own sentences.

1. might go We might go to North Carolina in December.
2. was sleeping I was sleeping when you called.
3. have stopped We have stopped working for today.

© Carson Dellosa CD-3742 30

Name ______________________ **Past Tense Verbs**

To tell something that has already happened, **-ed** is added to most verbs. This form of the verb is called the **past tense**.

Examples: My friends and I play outside a lot.
Yesterday, we played outside for three hours.

Rewrite each sentence in the past tense. The first one has been done for you.

1. I need a snack. *I needed a snack.*
2. I like cold milk. I liked cold milk.
3. The cookies look good. The cookies looked good.
4. The snack tastes great. The snack tasted great.
5. My dog plays with dirt. My dog played with dirt.
6. He chews on his bone. He chewed on his bone.
7. I laugh at his tricks. I laughed at his tricks.

Complete the sentences below using the past tense.

1. Yesterday morning I played football.
2. In the afternoon I ate some lunch.
3. I helped my mother cook dinner last night.
4. I talked on the phone before I went to sleep.
5. Joe fixed the broken pedal on his bicycle.

© Carson-Dellosa CD-3742 31

Name ______________________ **Past Tense Verbs**

To tell something that already happened, **-ed** is added to most verbs. This form of the verb is called the **past tense**.

Examples: My friends and I play outside a lot.
Yesterday we played outside for three hours.

Use the word bank to complete the past tense sentences below.

1. Timmy opened his mouth and yawned.
2. The baby screamed for her bottle.
3. Marlene spilled her popcorn.
4. Bob walked out the door an hour ago.
5. Gary played with his toy during the show.

WORD BANK

spilled	walked	played	screamed	yawned

Rewrite each sentence below, changing it to the past tense.

1. Don and Cal want to go to the movies. Don and Cal wanted to go to the movies.
2. They ask their parents. They asked their parents.
3. The two boys walk to the neighborhood theater. The two boys walked to the neighborhood theater.

© Carson-Dellosa CD-3742 32

Answer Key

Name ______________________ **Irregular Past Tense Verbs**

Some verbs do not form the past tense by adding -d or -ed. They form the past tense in other ways. These verbs are called **irregular verbs**.

Examples: I eat pizza every day. I ate pizza last night. Mary buys candy at the store. Mary bought candy yesterday.

Draw lines to match the present and past tense verb forms.

GROUP 1		GROUP 2	
take	threw	write	swam
give	went	drink	ran
choose	took	bring	drank
throw	rode	come	wrote
go	chose	swim	came
ride	gave	run	brought

Use past tense verbs from the above lists to complete each sentence.

1. We took my little brother to the zoo.
2. He brought along his stuffed bear.
3. First we all rode the zoo train.
4. Then we went to the monkey house.
5. We gave peanuts to the monkeys.
6. Next we saw some seals who swam in a big pool.
7. My friend said "Let's race," so we ran to the snack bar.

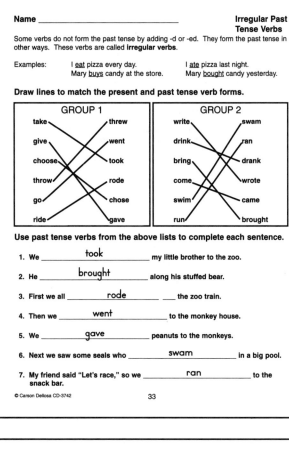

Name ______________________ **Irregular Past Tense Verbs**

Some verbs do not form the past tense by adding -d or -ed. They form the past tense in other ways. These verbs are called **irregular verbs**.

Examples: I wear shorts in summer. I wore shorts yesterday. Jim sells candy bars. Jim sold three candy bars.

Draw lines to match the present and past tense verb forms.

GROUP 1		GROUP 2	
fall	told	make	began
go	knew	eat	felt
break	fell	think	ate
sit	went	begin	forgave
know	sat	feel	made
tell	broke	forgive	thought

Use past tense verbs from the above lists to complete the story.

When I babysat my sister, I thought we would have a fun day. The day began fine. Then things got worse. My sister fell down on the sidewalk. Then I broke her piece of chalk accidentally. I felt bad. I told my sister that I was sorry and she forgave me. Then, we went into the house and watched a movie.

Name ______________________ **Verb Review**

In each blank, write the past tense form of the verbs to complete the story.

The camera was invented (invent) in the 1800s. A French scientist took (take) the first photograph in 1826. Cameras improved (improve) over the next 50 years, but only a few people had (have) their own cameras. Then an inventor named George Eastman had (have) an idea. He produced (produce) a simple, less-expensive camera and sold (sell) it to ordinary people. Many people bought (buy) Eastman's camera. After they took (take) a roll of film, they sent (send) it to Eastman's company where workers developed (develop) it. Eastman's company said (say), "You press the button, we do the rest."

Write your own sentences about a camera, using these past tense verbs.

1. flashed When we took the picture, the bulb flashed.
2. clicked The film clicked as it wound up.
3. took My mother took a lot of pictures at the party.

Name ______________________ **Verb Review**

The words below are all verbs. Circle every one that you have already done today. Then underline every one that you think you will do later today.

(BRUSH)	(DRINK)	(WALK)	(THINK)	FIX
(EAT)	DRIVE	(RIDE)	(WAKE)	KICK
(DRESS)	CLIMB	BOUNCE	FORGET	CRY
LAUGH	WRITE	MAKE	COOK	(READ)
BAKE	SKATE	REST	(PRAY)	(HOLD)
SING	CALL	FROWN	GIVE	HUG
(USE)	(SMILE)	JUMP	(STAND)	PAY
WAVE	(TALK)	PAINT	STUDY	SLEEP

Think of two OTHER verbs that you have done today.

loved saw

Answer these verb riddles:

I am something you might do when you are sad. What verb am I?

cry

I am something a dog does to make noise. What verb am I?

bark

I am what you are doing when you go off a board into the swimming pool. What verb am I?

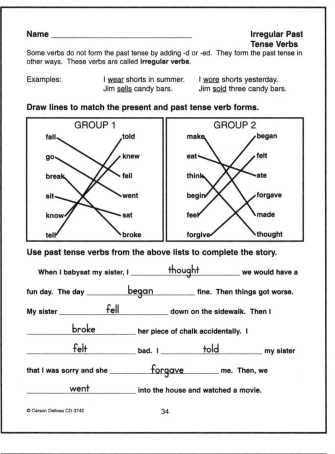

dive

Answer Key

Name ______________________ **Recognizing Adjectives**

An **adjective** is a word that describes a noun. Adjectives tell facts like *what kind, which one, how much,* or *how many.*

Examples: What kind: tall mountain, red shirt, ripe fruit, short nap
Which one: Boston Harbor, this boy, these books, the other game
How much/How many: two grapes, few answers, many bugs, no gum

Circle the adjective that describes each underlined noun in the sentences below.

1. An (important) statue stands in New York Harbor.
2. (This) statue was a gift to the United States from France.
3. It was built by a (young) sculptor named Auguste Bartholdi.
4. The United States built the (big) pedestal on which the statue stands.
5. Together the statue and the pedestal are a monument to freedom for the (two) nations.
6. It took over (two hundred) crates to ship the (huge) statue from France to New York.
7. Today (many) people still visit this (famous) statue.
8. What is (this) monument's name? The Statue of Liberty!

Rewrite the sentences below, adding an adjective to describe each underlined noun. (Example: A boat took us to the statue. A big boat took us to the incredible Statue.)

1. The statue is on the island. The enormous statue is on the small island.
2. My family went inside the statue. My friend's family went inside the beautiful statue.

 37

Name ______________________ **Recognizing Adjectives**

An **adjective** is a word that describes a noun. Adjectives tell facts like *what kind, which one, how much,* or *how many.*

Examples: What kind: deep ocean, white coat, heavy rocks, quick trip
Which one: Italian food, this cat, these flowers, final race
How much/How many: two grapes, a few trees, many bugs, no gum

Circle the adjective that describes each underlined noun in the sentences below. (Hint: A few nouns have more than one adjective—can you find them?)

1. Have you ever wondered what materials make up our (amazing) Earth?
2. The (first) layer inside Earth is called the crust.
3. The (hard), (rocky) crust is like a shell around the Earth.
4. Underneath the crust are (three) layers of rocks and metals.
5. The mantle is (1,800) miles thick and is made of (heavy) rocks.
6. In (some) places, the mantle is so hot that the rocks melt!
7. The next layer of Earth is the (outer) core.
8. The outer core contains (hot), (melted) rock.
9. The (inner) core is at the center of Earth.
10. (Two) types of metal, iron and nickel, make up the (solid) core.

Rewrite the sentences below, adding an adjective to describe each underlined noun.

1. Earth is a planet. Our Earth is a fascinating planet.
2. Scientists study Earth. Many scientists study inner Earth.

 38

Name ______________________ **Recognizing Adjectives**

An **adjective** is a word that describes a noun. Adjectives tell facts like *what kind, which one, how much,* or *how many.*

Examples: What kind: friendly girl, green tree, cold ice cream
Which one: that car, those videos, last game
How much/How many: five bees, few bites, some toes, no mice

Write an adjective to describe each noun. Then write a sentence using both nouns and their adjectives.

1. Your mother green vegetables
   Your mother cooks green vegetables.
2. That airplane young children
   That airplane is full of young children.
3. brown bear big forest
   The brown bear lived in the big forest.
4. green hat old man
   My green hat is on the old man.
5. science book torn page
   My science book has a torn page.
6. Her face pretty smile
   Her face has a pretty smile.
7. blue room tile floor
   The blue room has a tile floor.

 39

Name ______________________ **Recognizing Adjectives**

An **adjective** is a word that describes a noun. Adjectives tell facts like *what kind, which one, how much,* or *how many.*

Examples: What kind: The shiny, metal object looked like gold!
Which one: These pieces of metal are gold!
How much/How many: This gold is worth a thousand dollars!

In the paragraph below, circle the adjectives that describe each underlined noun.

How the Gold Rush Began

In 1848 a (young) carpenter named James Marshall made an (important) discovery that sent (many) Americans rushing to California. On January 24th, Marshall stopped his (carpentry) work to take a quiet walk along the river. Looking into the (clear) (blue) water, Marshall saw a (shiny), (yellow) object. As he bent down, he saw more (gleaming) objects. Marshall felt the (soft) metal. Could this be gold? He ran to tell his boss, John Sutter. What Marshall had found that day was gold. With his (exciting) discovery, the (California) Gold Rush began.

Complete the story using your own adjectives.

I love my little puppy. We bought him at the pet store in the mall. His eyes are brown, his fur is brown, and his ears are floppy. He loves to run across our back yard. We have a lot of fun together.

 40

Answer Key

Name ____________________ **Recognizing Adjectives**

Words that describe (tell more about) people, places and things are called **adjectives**. Sometimes adjectives come after the noun they describe, usually after linking verbs like *am, is, are, was,* and *were.*

Examples: I am sleepy. The grass is tall. My parents are kind. John was happy.

Underline the adjectives in the sentences below. Circle the noun they describe. The first one has been done for you.

1. Herman is huge and hairy.
2. The saleslady was polite.
3. Those brownies are delicious.
4. My grandparents are loving and kind.
5. Yesterday the clouds were big and puffy.
6. I was surprised by my party.
7. I am hungry.
8. The tulips are yellow and red.

Use the two adjectives listed below in a sentence. Write the sentence so that the adjectives come after the verb. The first one has been done for you.

1. tall and green *The fir trees were tall and green.*
2. quiet and peaceful Today the beach was quiet and peaceful.
3. long and wide The bridge is long and wide.
4. large and yellow Sheila's pencil is large and yellow.

Name ____________________ **Adjective Comparison**

To compare two nouns, use the comparative form of the adjective. This is formed by adding **-er** to most adjectives. When using adjectives of three or more syllables, you can usually add the word **more** before the adjective.
To compare three or more nouns, use the superlative form of the adjective. This is formed by adding **-est** to most adjectives. When using adjectives of three or more syllables add the word **most** in front of the adjective.

Examples: That silver trumpet is louder than the gold one. It is the loudest trumpet I have ever heard.

The red dress was more beautiful than the green one. It was the most beautiful dress I had ever seen.

Write the comparative and superlative forms of each adjective. The first one has been done for you.

Adjective	Comparative	Superlative
1. fast	faster	fastest
2. tall	taller	tallest
3. strong	stronger	strongest
4. smart	more thankful	most thankful
5. generous	more generous	most generous
6. quick	quicker	quickest
7. old	older	oldest
8. wise	more cautious	most cautious
9. delicate	more delicate	most delicate
10. high	higher	highest

Name ____________________ **Adjective Comparison**

To compare two nouns, use the comparative form of the adjective. This is formed by adding **-er** to most adjectives. When using adjectives of three or more syllables, you can usually add the word **more** before the adjective.
To compare three or more nouns, use the superlative form of the adjective. This is formed by adding **-est** to most adjectives. When using adjectives of three or more syllables add the word **most** in front of the adjective.

Examples: The basket is heavier than the box. It is the heaviest basket I've ever carried.

Dan is more courageous than Jim. Dan is the most courageous person I know.

Circle the better sentence in each pair.

1. ~~The first gymnast was skillfuler than the second one.~~
   The first gymnast was more skillful than the second one.
2. Zack's yell was the loudest of all.
   ~~Zack's yell was the most loud of all.~~
3. The big pine tree was older than the fir tree.
   ~~The big pine tree was more old than the fir tree.~~
4. ~~That was the incrediblest bubble I've ever blown!~~
   That was the most incredible bubble I've ever blown!
5. After the slumber party, Mary was sleepier than Leann.
   ~~After the slumber party, Mary was more sleepy than Leann.~~
6. ~~June was confidenter than Jane that she would pass the test.~~
   June was more confident than Jane that she would pass the test.
7. The newborn puppies were smaller than their mothers.
   ~~The newborn puppies were more small than their mothers.~~
8. ~~The Grand Tetons are the magnificentest mountains I have ever seen.~~
   The Grand Tetons are the most magnificent mountains I have ever seen.

Name ____________________ **Adjective Comparison**

The adjective **good** has special forms for comparison. To compare two things, the word **better** is used. To compare more than two things, the word **best** is used.

Examples: The apple pie was good. The cherry pie was better than the apple pie. The blueberry pie was the best pie of all.

The adjective **bad** has special forms for comparison also. To compare two things, the word **worse** is used. To compare more than two things the word **worst** is used.

Examples: That shampoo has a bad smell. That shampoo smells worse than a skunk! That is the worst smelling shampoo ever!

Choose the correct form of good or bad to complete each sentence.

1. That was the best baseball game I've seen all year. (good / better / best)
2. I think asparagus is worse than lima beans. (bad / worse / worst)
3. That camera takes the worst pictures I've ever seen. (bad / worse / worst)
4. Ben's skis are worse than Jan's. (bad / worse / worst)
5. The flu is worse than a cold. (bad / worse / worst)
6. The chicken pox is the worst illness I've ever had. (bad / worse / worst)
7. My pen is better than Mary's pen. (good / better / best)
8. Nick has better shoes for soccer than Lance. (good / better / best)

Answer Key

Name ______________________ **Articles**

Articles are small words that come before nouns or noun phrases. **A**, **an** and **the** are articles. **A** is used before a word that begins with a consonant. **An** is used before a word that begins with a vowel. Use **the** before a noun that names a particular person, place, or thing.

Examples:
an ocean
a continent
The earth is tilted a little bit.
The weather today is warm.

Write the correct article (*a or an*) before the noun or noun phrase.

1. a climate
2. an igloo
3. an ear
4. a lamp
5. a ray of sun
6. an ice cube
7. a satellite
8. an oven

Use articles (*a*, *an*, or *the*) to complete each sentence.

1. There is an imaginary line around the center of the earth that is called the equator.
2. The sun's rays shine most directly at the equator.
3. A climate is a pattern of weather in an area over a period of time.
4. A scientist who studies climate is a climatologist.

Name ______________________ **Adjective Review**

Find the adjective that describes the underlined noun in each sentence. Write it on the line.

fascinating 1. Australia is a fascinating country.
lot 2. It has a lot of land, but only 18 million people.
first 3. The aborigines were the first Australians.
Australian 4. The Australian continent is south of the equator.
opposite 5. Seasons south of the equator take place at opposite times of the year than they do north of the equator.
snow 6. In Australia, people can go snow skiing in July.
winter 7. They can sunbathe during our winter holidays.
unique 8. Unique animals live in Australia's outback.

Circle the adjectives that you find in each sentence. The number tells you how many there are.

1. Tasmania is the (smallest) state in Australia. (1)
2. Tasmania is an island off the (southern) coast of Australia. (1)
3. It is a (beautiful) island with (dense) forests and (wild) rivers. (3)
4. Tasmania used to be a (prison) colony. (1)
5. Now (many) tourists come to (this) island. (2)
6. (Some) visitors take bushwalks to see the (awesome) scenery. (2)

Name ______________________ **Recognizing Adverbs**

An **adverb** is a word that describes a verb. Adverbs tell *where, when, how,* or *to what extent* (how much or how long).

Examples:
The boat is leaving now. (When?)
My horse fell down. (Where?)
Paul worked busily. (How?)
William rode for days. (How long?)

Circle the adverb in each sentence. Underline the verb it describes.

1. Paul Revere and William Dawes rode (secretly.)
2. The people of Lexington awoke (early.)
3. They arose (quickly.)
4. The British soldiers marched (ahead.)
5. Shots were fired (somewhere.)
6. The colonists fought (bravely.)
7. The Battle of Lexington ended (quickly.)
8. The Revolutionary War began (here.)

Underline each adverb in the paragraph below. (There are six).

"The Shot Heard 'Round the World"

The British soldiers marched forward to Concord. The colonists' war supplies were stored there. The war supplies were destroyed, but the colonists fought long and hard. The British had to turn back to Boston. The Battle of Concord will be remembered forever in American history.

Name ______________________ **Recognizing Adverbs**

An **adverb** is a word that describes a verb. Adverbs *tell where, when, how,* or *to what extent* (how much or how long).

Examples:
The ticket booth opens now. (When?)
The line starts here. (Where?)
We petted the animals gently. (How?)
The baboons howled endlessly. (How long?)

Complete the sentences below, using an adverb from the adverb bank.

ADVERB BANK

When	Where	How	How much or How Long
daily	away	sloppily	often
now	down	carefully	never
usually	here	softly	forever
sometimes	nearby	secretly	far

1. The zookeeper feeds the animals daily.
2. The monkeys eat their food sloppily.
3. Lions eat the grass. The vultures wait nearby.
4. The zookeeper never forgets to feed the animals.
5. We watch secretly while the koala eats his bamboo.

Write four sentences using the adverb given.

1. (usually) We usually go to bed at 8:oo.
2. (here) We like to sit here.
3. (softly) Maria spoke softly.
4. (forever) She takes forever to get ready.

Answer Key

Name ________________ **Recognizing Adverbs**

An **adverb** is a word that describes a verb. Adverbs tell *where, when, how* or *to what extent* (how much or how long).

Examples: The 100 meter dash starts tomorrow. (When?)
That runner fell down. (Where?)
The ticket-takers worked quickly. (How?)
Marathon runners run far. (How long?)

Circle the adverb in each sentence. Underline the verb it describes.

1. We drove excitedly to Atlanta, Georgia.
2. The 1996 Olympic Games were there.
3. At the track and field events, contestants ran fast and jumped.
4. Gymnasts moved gracefully.
5. At the swimming pool, swimmers glided swiftly through the water.
6. Then the divers gave a show.
7. They dove down into the deep water.
8. Maybe if I work hard I can be in the Olympics.

Write your own sentences about sports using the adverbs listed.

1. carefully Please drive carefully.
2. tomorrow We will leave tomorrow.
3. outside Do not go outside.
4. quickly She left quickly.

© Carson Dellosa CD-3742 49

Name ________________ **Recognizing Adverbs**

An **adverb** is a word that describes a verb. Adverbs tell *where, when, how,* or *to what extent* (how much or how long).

Examples: You can have a snack later. (When?)
Are there cookies here? (Where?)
Mom makes cookies easily. (How?)
I never eat potato chips. (How much?)

Use your imagination to complete the story with adverbs. Remember, adverbs tell when, where, how, or to what extent (how much or how long).

News travels fast in my school. On the day I won 100 ice cream cone coupons, almost everybody was my friend. Marty came right up to me. She begged me for a chocolate cone. I told her shyly that I would think about it. Fernando came next. He got down on his knees and begged pitifully. Jill offered to trade me her bubble gum for a strawberry ice cream coupon, but I said "No, thanks." Wow, people sure act funny sometimes. I really do want to share my ice cream cones, I just want to wait first.

© Carson Dellosa CD-3742 50

Name ________________ **Recognizing Adverbs**

Circle the adverb that describes the underlined verb.

1. Our class went to Funtime Park yesterday.
2. A few of the girls ran immediately to the carousel.
3. James and I rode the roller coaster first.
4. James had never ridden a roller coaster before.
5. The car climbed slowly up the track.
6. Then we plunged downward.
7. Bill and I screamed loudly.
8. You may think we really hated our ride.
9. Not at all. We rode it again!
10. This time we rode fearlessly in the front seat.

Think of an adverb to describe each verb.

ran slowly turned around
ate hungrily shouted loudly

Use the verbs and adverbs from above to write four sentences.

1. I ran slowly and lost the race.
2. I turned around and there she was.
3. He ate hungrily, as if he had not eaten in days.
4. If you want to be heard, you must shout loudly.

© Carson Dellosa CD-3742 51

Name ________________ **Parts of Speech**

Match the parts of speech you have learned with their definitions.

D 1. Noun A) tells what is happening in the sentence
A 2. Verb B) describes a verb
C 3. Adjective C) describes a noun
B 4. Adverb D) names a person, place, or thing

Find parts of speech in the sentences below and write them on the lines.

1. These berries smash easily.
Noun berries Adjective These
Verb smash Adverb easily

2. Ten soldiers march together.
Noun soldiers Adjective Ten
Verb march Adverb together

3. The big pillow belongs here.
Noun pillow Adjective big
Verb belongs Adverb here

4. Round balls bounce nicely.
Noun balls Adjective Round
Verb bounce Adverb nicely

© Carson Dellosa CD-3742 52

Answer Key

Name ______________________ **Word Order**

Changing the **order of words** in a sentence can change the meaning.

Example: *Kangaroos are bigger than elephants.*
Elephants are bigger than kangaroos.
Both sentences have the same words, but in a different order.
Only one of the sentences states a fact.

For each pair of sentences below, circle the one that is correct.

1. The Earth travels around the Sun. (circled)
   The Sun travels around the Earth.
2. A man becomes a boy.
   A boy becomes a man. (circled)
3. A coconut is bigger than a lemon. (circled)
   A lemon is bigger than a coconut.
4. Flowers get pollen from bees.
   Bees get pollen from flowers. (circled)
5. Dogs are a kind of animal. (circled)
   Animals are a kind of dog.
6. Horses are faster than airplanes.
   Airplanes are faster than horses. (circled)
7. A circle is round and a square has four sides. (circled)
   A square is round and a circle has four sides.
8. Apples grow on trees. (circled)
   Trees grow on apples.
9. The equator is north of Canada.
   Canada is north of the equator. (circled)
10. The Earth lived on dinosaurs long ago.
    Dinosaurs lived on the earth long ago. (circled)

Name ______________________ **Statements**

A statement is a sentence that tells something. Statements begin with a capital letter and end with a period (.).

Examples of statements: The Netherlands is a beautiful country.
The Netherlands has a queen.

Not statements: What kind of money do Dutch people use?
Look at all the canals!

Write S on the line if the sentence is a statement.

S 1. I like to go swimming during the summer.
_____ 2. Is your name Fred?
S 3. My friend is the girl in the red shirt.
S 4. Yesterday we ate pizza for dinner.
_____ 5. Are you going to the party?
_____ 6. Yikes, that must have hurt!

Rewrite each statement correctly below. Remember to capitalize the first word and end each sentence with a period.

1. my family worked in the yard all day
   My family worked in the yard all day.
2. howard always tells the truth
   Howard always tells the truth.
3. soccer is a fun game
   Soccer is a fun game.

Name ______________________ **Questions**

A **question** is a sentence that asks something. A question begins with a capital letter and ends with a question mark (?).

Examples: What is your favorite sport?
Do you like to play it or watch it?

Write Q on the blank if the sentence is a question.

Q 1. Do you like to watch basketball games?
_____ 2. I think basketball games are exciting.
Q 3. What is double-dribbling?
_____ 4. Look out for that ball!
Q 5. Why are some shots worth three points?
_____ 6. The first basketball hoops were peach baskets hung up on a wall.

Rewrite each question correctly below. Remember to capitalize the first word and end each sentence with a question mark.

1. who invented basketball
   Who invented basketball?
2. how long does a game last
   How long does a game last?
3. what is a free throw
   What is a free throw?
4. where did you learn to play basketball
   Where did you learn to play basketball?

Name ______________________ **Exclamations**

An **exclamation** is a sentence that shows excitement or a strong feeling. An exclamation starts with a capital letter and ends with an exclamation point **(!)**. An exclamation may be only one or two words long.

Examples: I can't believe it! Wow, this is great!
Look out! It's so hot outside!

Write EX on the blank if the sentence is an exclamation.

EX 1. Whee, here we go!
EX 2. This water slide is great!
_____ 3. The water at the bottom is pretty cold.
_____ 4. Did you try slide number three?
EX 5. Wait till Ben hears about this place!
EX 6. Here I go!

Rewrite each exclamation correctly below. Remember to capitalize the first word and end each sentence with an exclamation mark.

1. summer's finally here
   Summer's finally here!
2. hooray for you
   Hooray for you!
3. let's go swimming
   Let's go swimming!
4. watch me dive
   Watch me dive!

Answer Key

Name ______________________ **Commands**

Commands are sentences that tell someone to do something. Strong commands end with exclamation points **(!)**.

Examples: Put the baby down. I said "NO!" Clean your room now! Watch out!

Write each command correctly on the line. Each is a strong command.

1. **fasten your seat belt**
   Fasten your seatbelt!
2. **be careful**
   Be careful!
3. **lock the door**
   Lock the door!
4. **don't litter**
   Don't litter!
5. **try again**
   Try again!
6. **stop whining**
   Stop whining!

Can you think of three commands someone has given you in the last week? Write them below.

1. Eat your breakfast!
2. Do your homework!
3. Clean up your room!

© Carson Dellosa CD-3742 57

Name ______________________ **Types of Sentences Review**

On the blank write S if the sentence is a statement, Q if it is a question, EX if it is an exclamation, and C if it is a command.

Q 1. **Is there always this much water falling?**
EX 2. **What an amazing view!**
Q 3. **What causes a waterfall?**
S 4. **These waterfalls are named Niagara Falls.**
EX 5. **I see a rainbow!**
C 6. **Watch out!**
S 7. **Niagara Falls are on the border of the United States and Canada.**
Q 8. **Can you see the falls from both countries?**
C 9. **Stand back from the edge!**
EX 10. **Look at all the people!**

Make your own sentences! Complete your own statement, question, exclamation, and command. Don't forget to use the correct punctuation.

1. **I think** it might rain.
2. **Do you** think it might rain?
3. **Wow,** it's raining!
4. **Never** play golf in the rain!

© Carson Dellosa CD-3742 58

Name ______________________ **Types of Sentences Review**

On the blank write S if the sentence is a statement, Q if it is a question, EX if it is an exclamation, and C if it is a command.

Q 1. **How big is the Sun?**
EX 2. **Wow, that is beautiful!**
Q 3. **How fast does the Earth travel around the Sun?**
S 4. **The Earth is 93 million miles from the Sun.**
EX 5. **That's farther than I can imagine!**
C 6. **Watch out—don't look directly at the Sun!**
S 7. **The Sun is an enormous ball of burning gas.**
Q 8. **Can satellites take pictures of the Sun?**
EX 9. **Nothing can get too close to the Sun!**
C 10. **Put that sun screen on now!**

Make your own sentences! Complete your own statement, question, exclamation, and command. Don't forget to use the correct punctuation.

1. **The Sun** Is bright.
2. **Are you** crazy?
3. **Hey,** this is amazing!
4. **Always** be careful when crossing the street!

© Carson Dellosa CD-3742 59

Name ______________________ **Subjects**

The **subject** of a sentence tells who or what the sentence is about. The **simple subject** is the noun that the sentence is about. The **complete subject** includes the words that tell more about the subject.

Examples: **Painting and sculpting** are two forms of art. **Some sculptors** model out of clay. **I** like to carve wood.

Circle the simple subject. Underline the complete subject.

1. **Many painters use different styles.**
2. **One style of painting is called Impressionism.**
3. **The art called impressionism began in France around 1875.**
4. **Claude Monet is considered the first impressionist painter.**
5. **His famous paintings were full of light.**
6. **The impressionists' goal was to capture light in their pictures.**
7. **Renoir and Pissarro are other famous impressionist painters.**
8. **Mary Cassatt, a female artist, brought Impressionism to America.**
9. **This woman is especially famous for her pictures of mothers and children.**
10. **Many people enjoy the impressionists' paintings in museums.**

Write your own simple or complete subject for each sentence.

1. Listening to your parents **is a wise thing to do.**
2. Many people **mow the grass.**
3. All the students **study for the test.**
4. The swimmers **practice hard every day.**

© Carson Dellosa CD-3742 60

Answer Key

Name ______________________ **Subjects**

The **subject** of a sentence tells who or what the sentence is about. The **simple subject** is the noun that the sentence is about. The **complete subject** includes the words that tell more about the subject.

Examples: **A *ship* with red and white sails** moved across the water.
It was a Viking ship.
***Eric the Red*, a famous Viking**, captained the ship.

Circle the simple subject. Write the complete subject of the sentence on the line.

1. A (group) of bold seamen lived in northern Europe 1000 years ago.
   A group of bold seamen
2. These (men) were called the Vikings.
   These men
3. The (Vikings) loved adventure.
   The Vikings
4. (They) sailed the oceans in beautifully painted ships.
   They
5. (Eric the Red) was a Viking leader.
   Eric the Red
6. (He) led the Vikings across the "Sea of Darkness."
   He
7. The ("Sea of Darkness") is what they called the Atlantic Ocean.
   The "Sea of Darkness"
8. These (seamen) sailed to Iceland and then to Greenland.
   These seamen

Name ______________________ **Predicates**

The **predicate** is the part of a sentence that tells something about the subject. The **simple predicate** is the verb. The **complete predicate** includes words that tell more about the verb.

Examples: The earth **has seven continents.**
The United States **is in North America**.

Circle the simple predicate. Write the complete predicate on the line.

1. The largest continent (is) Asia.
   is Asia
2. Russia, China, and India (are) in Asia.
   are in Asia
3. Europe (is connected) to Asia.
   is connected to Asia
4. Europe (is) the smallest continent.
   is the smallest continent
5. Some continents (have) many countries.
   have many countries
6. Australia (is) a continent and a country.
   is a continent and a country
7. Many small countries (are) on the continent of Africa.
   are on the continent of Africa

Complete each sentence by writing your own predicate.

1. One continent is North America.
2. Antarctica is a very cold place.

Name ______________________ **Predicates**

The **predicate** is the part of a sentence that tells something about the subject. The **simple predicate** is the verb. The **complete predicate** includes words that tell more about the verb.

Examples: The Middle Ages ***happened*** **1000 years ago**.
It ***was*** **the time of knights and noblemen.**

Circle the simple predicate. Underline the complete predicate.

1. People in Europe long ago (lived) on manors.
2. A manor (was) the land that belonged to a nobleman.
3. The nobleman (ruled) all of the people on his land.
4. A rich nobleman (might have) a castle on his land.
5. Castles (were) cold, damp, and dark.
6. There (was) also much farmland on a manor.
7. Peasants (were) the people who farmed the nobleman's land.
8. Peasants (worked) very hard.
9. They (lived) in small huts with dirt floors.
10. No peasants (could read) or write.
11. Very few noblemen (learned) to read or write.

Complete each sentence by writing your own predicate.

1. The life of a nobleman was easier than the life of a peasant.
2. The life of a peasant was a hard life.
3. I would not like to be a peasant.

Name ______________________ **Subjects & Predicates**

Every sentence has two parts: the subject and the predicate. The subject tells who or what the sentence is about. The predicate tells something about the subject.

Examples: My grandpa (Subject) works in his garden every day (Predicate).
Tulips and daffodils (Subject) are blooming in his yard (Predicate).

Match each subject on the left with a predicate on the right to make a complete sentence. Write the sentences below.

SUBJECTS	**PREDICATES**
The pink rose	is Mrs. Payne.
Last night's thunderstorm	smells wonderful.
My teacher's name	scared my little sister.
Milton	is our mailman.

1. The pink rose smells wonderful.
2. Last night's thunderstorm scared my little sister.
3. My teacher's name is Mrs. Payne.
4. Milton is our mailman.

Write your own subject to complete each sentence below.

1. My brother eats pancakes and sausage every day.
2. We like biscuits and jam.

Write your own predicate to complete each sentence below.

1. Jack and Jill went up the hill.
2. Little Red Riding Hood wore a red coat.

Answer Key

Name ______________________ **Subjects & Predicates**

Every sentence has two parts: the subject and the predicate. The subject tells who or what the sentence is about. The predicate tells something about the subject.

Examples: Camping (Subject) is fun when there are no bugs (Predicate).
The big owls (Subject) hooted all night long (Predicate).

In each sentence below, underline the complete subject once and the complete predicate twice.

1. Dad and I took our first camping trip.
2. We had a great time.
3. Our tent was just the right size.
4. Swimming and fishing kept us busy.
5. Our campfire burned brightly.
6. Dad told me stories about his boyhood.
7. The mosquitoes weren't too bad.
8. Two raccoons tried to eat our food.

Write your own subject to complete each sentence below.

1. The thunder made a lot of noise at night.
2. My sister and I ate our popcorn.

Write your own predicate to complete each sentence below.

1. A grizzly bear came into our tent.
2. The other campers told the bear to leave.

© Carson Dellosa CD-3742 65

Name ______________________ **Combining Subjects**

When two short sentences have the same verb, you can combine the subjects with the word *and*. This makes one longer, more interesting sentence.

Examples: Thomas Edison was a great inventor.
Guglielmo Marconi was a great inventor.
Thomas Edison and Guglielmo Marconi were great inventors.

Combine the subjects in each pair of sentences. Write the new sentence on the line.

1. **Automobiles were great inventions. Airplanes were great inventions.**
   Automobiles and airplanes were great inventions.
2. **Charles Duryea experimented with cars. Henry Ford experimented with cars.**
   Charles Duryea and Henry Ford experimented with cars.
3. **The Model T was an early car. The Model A was an early car.**
   The Model T and the Model A were early cars.
4. **New roads were built for cars. New bridges were built for cars.**
   New roads and bridges were built for cars.
5. **Orville Wright invented the airplane. Wilbur Wright invented the airplane.**
   Orville and Wilbur Wright invented the airplane.
6. **Charles Lindbergh was a famous pilot. Amelia Earhart was a famous pilot.**
   Charles Lindbergh and Amelia Earhart were famous pilots.
7. **The automobile made travel faster and easier. The airplane made travel faster and easier.**
   The automobile and airplane made travel faster and easier.

© Carson Dellosa CD-3742 66

Name ______________________ **Combining Subjects**

When two short sentences have the same verb, you can combine the subjects with the word *and*. This makes one longer, more interesting sentence.

Example: Pumice is a type of rock.
Basalt is a type of rock.
Pumice and basalt are types of rock.

Use the words given to make one sentence that has two subjects. The first one has been done for you.

1. cars, trains *Cars and Trains are both fun ways to travel.*
2. airplanes, rockets Airplanes and rockets can take you to far away places.
3. stones, pebbles Stones and pebbles are fun to collect.
4. dogs, cats Dogs and cats can sometimes be friends.
5. table, chairs A table and chairs are a good thing to have.
6. trees, flowers Trees and flowers grow in my backyard.
7. wind, rain The wind and rain scared me.

© Carson Dellosa CD-3742 67

Name ______________________ **Combining Predicates**

When two short sentences have the same subject, but different verbs, you can combine the verbs with the word *and* or *but*. This makes one longer, more interesting sentence.

Examples: Many inventors work hard.
Many inventors never become famous.
Many inventors work hard, but never become famous.

Combine the predicates in each pair of sentences with the word given (*and* or *but*). Write the new sentence on the line.

1. **Thomas Edison was a school dropout. Thomas Edison became a great inventor. (but)**
   Thomas Edison was a school dropout, but became a great inventor.
2. **Young Edison worked as a telegraph operator. Young Edison planned his inventions. (and)**
   Young Edison worked as a telegraph operator and planned his inventions.
3. **Edison built his own laboratory. Edison hired some assistants. (and)**
   Edison built his own laboratory and hired some assistants.
4. **Edison invented the record player. Edison perfected the electric light. (and)**
   Edison invented the record player and perfected the electric light.
5. **Edison invented the voting machine. Edison invented the microphone. (and)**
   Edison invented the voting machine and the microphone.
6. **Edison did not invent television. Edison's discoveries helped make television possible. (but)**
   Edison did not invent the television, but helped make television possible.

© Carson Dellosa CD-3742 68

Answer Key

Name ______________________ **Combining Predicates**

When two short sentences have the same subject, but different verbs, you can combine the verbs with the word *and* or *but*. This makes one longer, more interesting sentence.

Examples: Turtles **live in water**.
Turtles **lay their eggs on land**.
Turtles **live in water but lay their eggs on land**.

Combine the predicates in each pair of sentences with the word given (*and* or *but*). Write the new sentence on the line.

1. **Anteaters eat bugs. Anteaters don't have any teeth. (but)**
   Anteaters eat bugs but don't have any teeth.
2. **I like to ride my bike. I like to go for walks. (and)**
   I like to ride my bike and go for walks.
3. **Molly loves the summer. Molly does not like the winter. (but)**
   Molly loves the summer but does not like the winter.
4. **The days are long in the summer. The days are short in the winter. (and)**
   The days are long in the summer but short in the winter.
5. **My house has four bedrooms. My house has two swimming pools. (and)**
   My house has four bedrooms and two swimming pools.
6. **Sometimes I don't like to study. I like to make good grades. (but)**
   Sometimes I don't like to study, but I like to make good grades.

Name ______________________ **Combining Sentences**

Sometimes two short sentences about the same topic can be combined into one more interesting sentence. Combine the sentences with a comma (,) and the words *and* or *but*.

Example: Trees shade our yards. They give us beauty.
Trees shade our yards, and they give us beauty.

Combine the two sentences using a comma and the word *and* or *but*. Write the new sentence on the line. The first one has been done for you.

1. **Trees have many parts. They are all important.**
   Trees have many parts, and they are all important.
2. **Roots anchor the tree to the ground. They take water from the soil.**
   Roots anchor the tree to the ground, and they take water from the soil.
3. **The trunk supports the tree. It gives the tree strength.**
   The trunk supports the tree, and it gives the tree strength.
4. **Some tree trunks are straight. Some are twisted.**
   Some tree trunks are straight, and some are twisted.
5. **Branches give the tree shape. They hold the leaves out to the sun.**
   Branches give the tree shape, and they hold the leaves out to the sun.
6. **Leaves are where the tree makes its food. Flowers are where the seeds grow.**
   Leaves are where the tree makes its food, and flowers are where the seeds grow.
7. **Some trees have big flowers. Others have flowers that are hard to see.**
   Some trees have big flowers, and others have flowers that are hard to see.
8. **Some seeds are protected by cones. Others are protected by fruit.**
   Some seeds are protected by cones, and others are protected by fruit.

Name ______________________ **Combining Sentences**

Sometimes two short sentences about the same topic can be combined into one more interesting sentence. Combine the sentences with a comma (,) and the words *and* or *but*.

Example: We saw many mushrooms. We didn't pick them.
We saw many mushrooms, but we didn't pick them.

Combine the two sentences using a comma and the word *and* or *but*. Write the new sentence on the line. The first one has been done for you.

1. **There are many kinds of mushrooms. Only some are edible.**
   There are many kinds of mushrooms, but only some are edible.
2. **Some mushrooms grow in meadows. Some grow on tree stumps.**
   Some mushrooms grow in meadows, and some grow on tree stumps.
3. **Some mushrooms taste sweet. Some are very peppery tasting.**
   Some mushrooms taste sweet, but some are very peppery tasting.
4. **Many people eat mushrooms in salads. They can also be cooked.**
   Many people eat mushrooms in salads, but they can also be cooked.
5. **Most poisonous mushrooms grow in the woods. They are sometimes hard to recognize.**
   Most poisonous mushrooms grow in the woods, and they are sometimes hard to recognize.
6. **A mushroom is a fungus. It feeds on other organisms.**
   A mushroom is a fungus, and it feeds on other organisms.
7. **Some mushrooms can be poisonous. Only trained collectors should gather them.**
   Some mushrooms can be poisonous, and only trained collectors should gather them.

Name ______________________ **Subject-Verb Agreement**

Verbs that are in the **present tense** (tell what is happening now) have two forms. Use the form that goes with the subject. When the subject is third person singular (he, she, it, Mary, the dog, Joe) the verb usually ends in **-s**.

Examples: Jed runs. The dog barks.

When the subject is not third person singular (I, you, we, they, the people) -**s** is usually not added.

Examples: They run. Fido and Rover bark.

Complete each sentence with the correct verb form.

1. **In the summer, I** ___work___ **as a detective.** (work / works)
2. **I** ___solve___ **neighborhood mysteries.** (solve / solves)
3. **When Mrs. Carter** ___loses___ **her cat, I help her find it.** (lose / loses)
4. **If there are footprints, I** ___find___ **out whose they are.** (find / finds)
5. **My friend Jim** ___writes___ **me secret messages.** (write / writes)
6. **I** ___use___ **my decoder to figure them out.** (use / uses)
7. **I** ___keep___ **my detective kit in a secret place.** (keep / keeps)
8. **Only Mom and Dad** ___know___ **where it is.** (know / knows)
9. **Jim** ___wants___ **to be a neighborhood detective too.** (want / wants)
10. **Then we can** ___solve___ **mysteries together.** (solve / solves)

Answer Key

Name ______________________ Subject-Verb Agreement

Complete each sentence with the correct verb form.

1. Sound is what you hear (hear / hears) when air moves (move / moves) back and forth quickly, or vibrates (vibrate / vibrates).
2. All musical instruments make (make / makes) sound, but they make (make / makes) it in different ways.
3. When you press (press / presses) a piano key, a string vibrates (vibrate / vibrates) to make sound.
4. A guitar player strums (strum / strums) strings to make sound.
5. A wind instrument makes (make / makes) sound when someone blows (blow / blows) into it.
6. To make a trumpet sound, the musician blows (blow / blows) into the instrument and pushes (push / pushes) buttons.
7. Drums make (make / makes) sound when someone strikes (strike / strikes) them.

 73

Name ______________________ Sentence Fragments

A sentence is a group of words that tells a complete idea. A sentence begins with a capital letter and ends with a punctuation mark. When a sentence is left incomplete it is called a **fragment**.

Examples:

	Sentence	There are many kinds of storms.
	Fragment	Kinds of storms.
	Sentence	Storms can be very powerful.
	Fragment	Can be very powerful.

Write S if the words below are a sentence and F if they are a fragment.

F 1. Blowing wildly and knocking down trees.
S 2. Lightning is a spark of electricity in the sky.
F 3. A very loud noise.
S 4. Thunder is a noise made when hot and cold air meet.
F 5. Powerful windstorm.
S 6. A tornado is shaped like a funnel.
S 7. Hurricanes are storms that start over oceans.
F 8. Called the eye of the storm.
S 9. Hurricanes are also called typhoons.
F 10. Predict the weather.

Add words of your own to make each phrase a sentence.

1. Rain storms are good for our grass.
2. Lightning struck our house yesterday.

 74

Name ______________________ Sentence Fragments

Write S if the words below are a sentence and F if they are a fragment.

S 1. There are many beautiful mountain ranges in the world.
S 2. The highest mountain chain is the Himalayas.
F 3. Stretch across much of Asia.
S 4. The Swiss and Austrian Alps have many wildflowers.
F 5. Perhaps the most famous mountains in the world.
S 6. Mont Blanc is Europe's highest mountain.
F 7. The Rocky Mountains and the Appalachian Mountains.
S 8. The Rockies run through western Canada and the United States.
F 9. Called the Appalachian Trail.
S 10. Mountains are a majestic, awesome sight.

Underline the fragments in the paragraph below.

In 1953 a group of explorers set off. To climb Mount Everest. Mount Everest is the world's highest mountain. Standing at 8,848 meters high. Edmund Hillary of New Zealand and Tenzing Norgay of Nepal were the only two men to reach the mountain's top. They edged up the final ice-covered rock on May 29, 1953. Stood at the top of the world.

 75

Name ______________________ Direct Objects

A noun or a pronoun that receives the action of the verb is called a **direct object**. Direct objects follow action verbs and answer the questions "What?" or "Whom?"

Examples:
My family watched the sunset. (Watched what?)
I like my grandmother. (Like whom?)
I like her. (Like whom?)

Circle the verb in each sentence. Then find the direct object and write it on the line. (Hint: When you find the verb, ask yourself the questions "What?" or "Whom?") The first one has been done for you.

farm 1. Uncle John (owns) a farm.
cows 2. Every day he (milks) the cows.
corn 3. He (plants) corn in the spring.
pigs 4. Uncle John (feeds) the pigs.
horses 5. He (takes) his horses to shows.
vegetables 6. Aunt Vivian (grows) vegetables.
tomatoes 7. She (cans) tomatoes every summer.
bread 8. She also (bakes) bread.

Complete each sentence by writing your own direct objects.

1. The horses eat hay.
2. The kittens drink milk.
3. I saw wheat on the farm.
4. The children help plant beans.

 76

Answer Key

Name ______________________ **Direct Objects**

A noun or a pronoun that receives the action of the verb is called a **direct object**. Direct objects follow action verbs and answer the questions "What?" or "Whom?"

Examples: I drove the car to the airport. (Drove what?)
I visited Uncle Pedro. (Visited whom?)
I like him. (Like whom?)

Circle the verb in each sentence. Then find the direct object and write it on the line. (Hint: When you find the verb, ask yourself the questions "What?" or "Whom?") The first one has been done for you.

people 1. In Mexico City you will see many people.
streets 2. Cars and buses crowd the streets.
smog 3. You may breathe smog there.
sights 4. You can also see beautiful sights.
tacos 5. You can eat tacos.
bullfight 6. You may even see a bullfight.
sombrero 7. You can buy a sombrero for your head.
ruins 8. Many tourists visit Aztec ruins.

Complete each sentence by writing your own direct objects.

1. I would like to visit Italy.
2. I would see the pope.
3. I might find a rock.
4. I would eat some pizza.

Name ______________________ **Word Usage**

ITS AND IT'S

Its is a possessive pronoun and does not have an apostrophe.

Example: That is my dog. Its fur is brown.

It's is a contraction for *it is* or *it has* and has an apostrophe.

Examples: It's a warm day today. (It is a warm day today.)
It's taken a long time. (It has taken a long time.)

Complete each sentence with either *its* or *it's*.

1. My kitty chased its tail.
2. It's almost time for the bell to ring.
3. The grizzly bear was looking for its cub.
4. Its leg is broken.
5. It's my favorite dessert.
6. It's the first door on the right.
7. Its petals are bright red.
8. The dog has eaten all of its food.

Write a sentence of your own using *its*.

Its fleece was white as snow.

Write a sentence of your own using *it's*.

It's a beautiful day in the neighborhood.

Name ______________________ **Word Usage**

WHOSE AND WHO'S

Whose is a possessive pronoun and does not have an apostrophe.

Example: Whose book is that?

Who's is a contraction for *who is* or *who has* and has an apostrophe.

Example: Who's going to the fair? (Who is going to the fair?)
Who's eaten my cookie? (Who has eaten my cookie?)

Complete each sentence with *whose* or *who's*.

1. Who's seen my lost pencil?
2. Whose pretty flowers are those?
3. Who's your favorite actor?
4. Whose bicycle is outside in the rain?
5. Who's on my baseball team?
6. Whose gloves are on the teacher's desk?
7. Whose dad can drive us to the hockey game?
8. Who's the kindest person you know?

Write sentences about your family and friends with *whose* and *who's*.

1. Who's Who's afraid of the big bad wolf?
2. Whose Whose coat is on the table?

Name ______________________ **Word Usage**

YOUR AND YOU'RE

Your is a possessive pronoun and does not have an apostrophe.

Example: Your book is on the table.

You're is a contraction for *you are* and has an apostrophe.

Example: You're the best gardener I know.

Complete each sentence with *your* or *you're*.

1. Is that your mom in the green van?
2. You're my closest friend.
3. Your speech was excellent!
4. Did you know that you're first in line?
5. You're going to be late for the bus!

Complete the paragraph using *your* or *you're*.

Is that your bicycle on the steps? You're going to be in trouble for leaving it outside in the rain. I bet your mom will be mad. What? You're just washing it with rainwater? Your car is getting washed too? Well I hope you're able to convince your mom that rainwater is good for bicycles.

Answer Key

Name ______________________ **Word Usage**

Knowing when to use *has* and *have* can be confusing. **Has** tells about one person, place or thing. **Have** is used with *I, you,* and with words that tell about more than one person, place, or thing.

Examples: Drew has a computer.
The computer has a monitor.
I have a computer.
You have a printer.
The teachers have computers.

Write the correct word (*has* or *have*) to complete each sentence.

1. Mrs. Peters has a collection of beautiful quilts.
2. The quilts have special places in her house.
3. Each quilt has its own colors and pattern.
4. One quilt has pink squares with flowers.
5. Mike Peters has a soccer quilt for his room.
6. Libby and Elena have new quilts for their beds.
7. The oldest quilt has hearts on it.
8. I don't have any quilts at my house.

Write a sentence using the word *has*.

Maria has brown hair.

Write a sentence using the word *have*.

I have blond hair.

© Carson Dellosa CD-3742 81

Name ______________________ **Word Usage**

Knowing when to use *don't* and *doesn't* can be confusing. **Don't** is used with plural subjects and with the pronouns *I* and *you*. **Doesn't** is used with subjects that tell about one person, place, or thing.

Examples: These flowers don't have a smell.
I don't know that song.
Don't these papers go in your folder?
Doesn't Margie like pizza?
My cat doesn't purr very often.
It doesn't take long to do my homework.

Write the correct word (*don't* or *doesn't*) to complete each sentence.

1. Our toaster doesn't work very well.
2. Some birds don't fly south for the winter.
3. You don't need to wake me up early tomorrow.
4. I sure don't miss the cold weather!
5. That tree doesn't have leaves; it has needles.
6. William doesn't like to swim very much.
7. The computer doesn't need a new monitor.
8. Don't you like my new bicycle?

Write a sentence using the word *don't*.

I don't like you.

Write a sentence using the word *doesn't*.

He doesn't know you.

© Carson Dellosa CD-3742 82

Name ______________________ **Word Usage**

GOOD OR WELL?

Good is an adjective and describes a noun or a pronoun.

Examples: That cake is really good. (*good* describes *cake*)
We had a good time at the beach. (*good* describes *time*)

Well is an adverb and describes a verb. Well can also be an adjective when it means "healthy."

Examples: Pam sang well. (How did Pam sing?)
Jerry feels well today. ("healthy")

Complete each sentence with *good* or *well*. Circle the word that good or well describes. The first one has been for you.

1. Mark can (play) chess very well.
2. The drums (sound) really good.
3. Our (meeting) went well.
4. Does Ashley (dance) as well as Sarah?
5. You (can get) good exercise with a jump rope.
6. The (strawberries) are good.
7. Can Tina (sing) well.
8. I had a good (time) at the party yesterday.
9. The swimming pool (feels) good in this hot weather.
10. Our class (did) well on the spelling test.

© Carson Dellosa CD-3742 83

Name ______________________ **Word Usage**

Words that are pronounced the same but have different spellings and different meanings are called **homonyms**.

Examples: The building is made of steel.
That robber plans to steal the diamonds.

Complete each sentence with the correct homonym.

1. The party will be here (hear / here).
   Can you hear (hear / here) what I am saying?
2. There were drops of dew (dew / do) on the grass.
   Do (dew / do) you know what time it is?
3. There are four (for / four) people in my family.
   What are we having for (for / four) supper?
4. I can see (see / sea) far from this tower.
   We took our sailboat out on the sea (see / sea).
5. Our math test is next week (week / weak).
   After running five miles I felt weak (week / weak).
6. I like plain (plane / plain) spaghetti.
   My cousin flies in his plane (plane / plain).

© Carson Dellosa CD-3742 84

Answer Key

Name ______________________ **Word Usage**

Words that are pronounced the same but have different spellings and different meanings are called **homonyms**.

Examples: The wind blew my umbrella.
My favorite color is blue.

Complete each sentence with the correct homonym.

1. **May I have a** piece (peace / piece) **of cake?**
   The war ended and peace (peace / piece) **returned.**
2. **There are** too (two / to / too) **many bunnies in this cage.**
   I have two (two / to / too) **pet bunnies.**
   I am going to (two / to / too) **the pet store.**
3. **Your book is** by (buy / by / bye) **the window.**
   Will you buy (buy / by / bye) **some milk at the store?**
   Please go tell Marie good bye (buy / by / bye).
4. There (there / their) **is a fly in my soup.**
   Is this their (there / their) **cat?**
5. **Ted dressed up as a** knight (knight / night).
   Last night (knight / night) **we went to the movies.**
6. **An octopus has** eight (ate / eight) **legs.**
   Calvin ate (ate / eight) **the last piece of pie.**

Name ______________________ **Word Usage**

A **negative** is a word that means "no". Here are some negative words: *no, not, none, never, no one, nothing* and the ending *-n't*. Use only ONE negative word in a sentence.

Examples:
Correct: We never go to the skating rink.
Incorrect: We don't never go to the skating rink.
Correct: We never have anything to do.
Incorrect: We never have nothing to do.

Each sentence below has two negatives. Rewrite it correctly on the line. The first one has been done for you.

1. **Pam hasn't never gone to the movies.**
   Pam hasn't ever gone to the movies.
2. **We didn't see no bears in the forest.**
   We didn't see any bears in the park.
3. **Jim never had no problems with his homework.**
   Jim never had any problems with his homework.
4. **The baker didn't have nothing left for me to buy.**
   The baker didn't have anything left for me to buy.
5. **Don't never leave the door open.**
   Don't ever leave the door open.
6. **Joey doesn't have none of those toys.**
   Joey doesn't have any of those toys.
7. **My mom can't find no sugar for the cake.**
   My mom can't find any sugar for the cake.
8. **I couldn't never lift that much weight!**
   I couldn't ever lift that much weight.

Name ______________________ **Capitalization**

Remember to use **capital letters** when writing these things:

1. the first word in a sentence
2. the pronoun I
3. proper nouns—names of particular people, places, or things
4. important words in titles (of books, stories, movies, etc.)

Each sentence below has one or more capitalization mistakes. Write each sentence correctly on the line below it.

1. **The name of my school is fairmont elementary.**
   The name of my school is Fairmont Elementary.
2. **my favorite teacher is mrs. elgin.**
   My favorite teacher is Mrs. Elgin.
3. **My friend mary and i like our geography class best.**
   My friend Mary and I like our geography class best.
4. **So far we have studied north america and europe.**
   So far we have studied North America and Europe.
5. **Now we are studying brazil, a country in south america.**
   Now we are studying Brazil, a country in South America.
6. **rio de janiero and sao paulo are two of brazil's big cities.**
   Rio de Janiero and Sao Paulo are two of Brazil's big cities.
7. **The amazon river flows through brazil.**
   The Amazon River flows through Brazil.
8. **i am reading a book called the amazon rainforest**
   I am reading a book called The Amazon Rainforest.

Name ______________________ **Capitalization**

Remember to use **capital letters** when writing these things:

1. the first word in a sentence
2. the pronoun *I*
3. proper noun—names of particular people, places, or things
4. important words in titles (of books, stories, movies, etc.)

Each sentence below has one or more capitalization mistakes. Write each sentence correctly on the line below it.

1. **paris is the capital city of france.**
   Paris is the capital city of France.
2. **The seine river flows through paris.**
   The Seine River flows through Paris.
3. **many people visit the eiffel tower.**
   Many people visit the Eiffel Tower.
4. **Paris has a famous church called notre dame.**
   Paris has a famous church called Notre Dame.
5. **Another place to visit is the louvre, a famous art museum.**
   Another place to visit is the Louvre, a famous art museum.
6. **brigitte and jacques live in paris.**
   Brigitte and Jacques live in Paris.
7. **Their poodle fifi lives with them.**
   Their poodle, Fifi, lives with them.
8. **i would like to visit this city in france someday.**
   I would like to visit this city in France someday

Answer Key

Name ______________________ **Titles**

The first word and all important words in a book title begin with a **capital letter**. Book titles are underlined when they are written.

Example: Where the Red Fern Grows is my favorite book.

Each sentence has a book title written in italics. Rewrite each book title with proper capitalization. Don't forget to underline the title!

1. **Last week I read *detective dan and the missing marble mystery*.**
   Last week I read Detective Dan and the Missing Marble Mystery.
2. **My little sister loves *read aloud bedtime stories*.**
   My little sister loves Read Aloud Bedtime Stories.
3. ***charlotte's web* is a story about friendship.**
   Charlotte's Web is a story about friendship.
4. ***the word detective* is a funny book about nouns and verbs.**
   The Word Detective is a funny book about nouns and verbs.
5. **My mom just read a famous novel called *jane eyre*.**
   My mom just read a famous novel called Jane Eyre.
6. **Dad always keeps *the world almanac* handy.**
   Dad always keeps The World Almanac handy.

Write the title of a book to answer each question.

1. **If you were to write a book, what would you title it?**
   The Day Pigs Flew
2. **Name one book that you would like to read.**
   The Hobbit

© Carson Dellosa CD-3742 89

Name ______________________ **Commas**

Commas (,) are used to separate words in a series (a list).

Example: Trees need sunlight, water, and carbon dioxide to make food.

Add commas where they are needed in the sentences below.

1. **Our air is composed of nitrogen, oxygen, and other gases.**
2. **Togas, kimonos, and saris are all types of clothing.**
3. **George Washington, John Adams, and Thomas Jefferson were the first three presidents of the United States.**
4. **Several parts of a knight's armor are the breastplate, the helmet, and the shield.**
5. **Yellowstone, Badlands Glacier, and Shenandoah are names of national parks.**
6. **Trumpets, trombones, and tubas are all brass instruments.**
7. **Louisa May Alcott wrote Little Women, Little Men, and Jo's Boys.**
8. **Science, Spanish, and American history are my favorite subjects to study.**

Write sentences using the words given in a series.

1. **red, yellow, and gold**
   Our school colors are red, yellow, and gold.
2. **rollerblades, skateboards, and bicycles**
   At this store they sell rollerblades, skateboards, and bicycles.

© Carson Dellosa CD-3742 90

Name ______________________ **Commas**

Commas (,) are used to separate words in a series (a list).

Example: Grapefruit, oranges, tangerines, and lemons are citrus fruits.

Rewrite each sentence below using commas where they are needed.

1. **Sally bought some milk eggs and cheese at the store.**
   Sally bought some milk, eggs, and cheese at the store.
2. **Please bring a pencil some paper and an eraser to school tomorrow.**
   Please bring a pencil, some paper, and an eraser to school tomorrow.
3. **When it's cold I wear my gloves scarf and hat.**
   When it's cold I wear my gloves, scarf, and hat.
4. **Good sources of protein are meat fish eggs soybeans and nuts.**
   Good sources of protein are meat, fish, eggs, soybeans, and nuts.
5. **Each morning Peter wakes up takes a shower and eats breakfast.**
   Each morning Peter wakes up, takes a shower, and eats breakfast.

© Carson-Dellosa CD-3742 91

Name ______________________ **Commas**

Commas are used to separate dates and years. Commas are used to separate cities and states.

Examples:	January 1, 1929 April 15, 1975	Baton Rouge, Louisiana Laramie, Wyoming

If the date or address is in the middle of a sentence, a comma also follows the year and the state.

Examples: On October 12, 1492, Columbus reached land.
We visited Jackson, Mississippi, on our vacation.

Put commas where they belong in the dates and places below.

March 23, 1995	**Blacksburg, Virginia**
May 8, 1967	**Chicago, Illinois**
August 5, 1876	**Fargo, North Dakota**
September 13, 1996	**Atlanta, Georgia**
December 25, 1913	**Needles, California**

Correct these sentences by putting commas where they are needed for dates and places.

1. **On July 4, 1776, the Declaration of Independence was accepted.**
2. **We visited Philadelphia, Pennsylvania and Baltimore, Maryland.**
3. **On March 12, 1996, our state will have an election.**
4. **We just moved from Canyonville, Oregon to Norwood, Massachusetts.**
5. **Did you know that on May 11, 1858, Minnesota became a state?**
6. **Enid, Oklahoma is a fine city to visit.**

© Carson Dellosa CD-3742 92

Answer Key

Name ______________________ **Contractions**

A **contraction** is two words that are put together to make one shorter word. One kind of contraction is made with a verb + not. An apostrophe is used in a contraction to show where letters have been left out.

Examples: can + not = can't; is + not = isn't; have + not = haven't; will + not = won't; do + not = don't; are + not = aren't; was + not = wasn't

Write each sentence on the line, changing the underlined words to a contraction.

1. I can not play ball this afternoon.
   I can't play ball this afternoon.
2. It just is not possible.
   It just isn't possible.
3. I do not have the time.
   I don't have the time.
4. I will not be able to play until my book report is done.
   I won't be able to play until my book report is done.

Write a sentence using each contraction.

1. can't
   I can't go with you.
2. aren't
   We aren't finished yet.
3. don't
   I don't think he is here.

Name ______________________ **Contractions**

A **contraction** is two words that are put together to make one shorter word. One kind of contraction is made with a pronoun + a verb. An apostrophe is used in a contraction to show where letters have been left out.

Examples: I + am = I'm; he + will = he'll; it + is = it's; I + would = I'd; you + will = you'll; we + are = we're; they + are = they're; I + have = I've

Match the words on the left with the contractions on the right.

1. D We are — A) He'd
2. B I will — B) I'll
3. E She is — C) There's
4. C There is — D) We're
5. A He would — E) She's

Complete the story by adding contractions made from the words below each line.

We're (We are) taking my dad to the airport today. He's (He is) going on a business trip to Washington, D.C., but he'll (he will) be back on Thursday. I'm (I am) always happy to go to the airport. It's (It is) such an exciting place! I hope I'll (I will) get to see some fighter jets. They're (They are) amazing. I've (I have) always wanted to ride in one.

Name ______________________ **Quotes**

Quotation marks (“ ”) are used when writing a person's exact words.

1. Put quotation marks before and after a person's words.
2. Use a comma, question mark, or exclamation point to separate the spoken words from the rest of the sentence.
3. Begin the quote (the spoken words) with a capital letter.

Examples: “We should get an animal,” I said. “Would you really like a pet?” said Mom. “Let's get a cat!” yelled my sister.

Add quotation marks where they belong in the sentences below.

1. “I think a dog would make a good pet,” I said.
2. “Dogs are loyal and smart,” replied Mom.
3. Then she asked, “What kind of dog would you like?”
4. “Let me think about it,” I answered.

Rewrite each sentence adding quotation marks and punctuation.

1. I found a book about dogs in the library I told Mom.
   “I found a book about dogs in the library,” I told mom.
2. I think a spaniel would be a good pet I said.
   “I think a spaniel would be a good pet,” I said.
3. But how big do they get she asked.
   “But how big do they get?” she asked.
4. They are medium-sized I replied.
   “They are medium-sized,” I replied.
5. Let's start looking for a spaniel declared Mom.
   “Lets start looking for a spaniel,” declared Mom.

Name ______________________ **Quotes**

Quotation marks (“ ”) are used when writing a person's exact words.

1. Put quotation marks before and after a person's words.
2. Use a comma, question mark or exclamation point to separate the spoken words from the rest of the sentence.
3. Begin the quote (the spoken words) with a capital letter.

Examples: “How was your vacation?” asked Ben. “I had a great time,” replied Kyle.

Add quotation marks and punctuation marks to the sentences below.

1. “I just went to the moon,” declared Kyle.
2. “No way,” stated Ben.
3. “Well, I went to a place like the moon,” said Kyle.
4. “It's called Craters of the Moon National Monument” he added.
5. “It's in Idaho, and we stopped there on our vacation,” said Kyle.
6. “Why is it called Craters of the Moon,” asked Ben.
7. “Lava from a volcano hardened into rock,” Kyle said.
8. “All you can see for miles around is bare rock covering the ground. It looks just like the moon.”
9. Ben laughed and said, “Maybe I'll go to the moon someday, too!”
10. “Until you do, you can look at my pictures and pretend with me,” said Kyle.

Write your own quote with quotation marks to answer the question.

What would you say if you really landed on the moon?

“Wow, this is neat!”

Answer Key

Name ______________________ **Proofreading**

Reading over your work to check it is called **proofreading**. Proofreading is important at school and also at home (like when you write a letter to a relative or friend).
When you proofread something you have written, check spelling, capital letters, punctuation marks and grammar (to see that you have used words correctly).

Examples:

BEFORE PROOFREADING	AFTER PROOFREADING
Did Tom name his puppy maverick.	Did Tom name his puppy *Maverick*?
We was going to the movies.	We *were* going to the movies.
"Please pass the peas, I said.	"Please pass the peas," I said.

Proofread each sentence below and draw a circle around the error or where something is missing. Write the sentence correctly on the line. (The number after the sentence tells how many mistakes can be found.)

1. kenya is a country in eastern africa. (2)
   Kenya is a country in Eastern Africa.
2. The indian ocean lies on the southeast coast of Kenya. (2)
   The Indian Ocean lies on the southeast coast of Kenya.
3. Does Kenya really have many wild cheetahs and lions. (1)
   Does Kenya really have many wild cheetahs and lions?
4. Mt. elgon National Park is a good plac to see elephants. (2)
   Mt. Elgon National Park is a good place to see elephants.
5. Many visitors goes exploring in Kenyas wildlife parks. (2)
   Many visitors go exploring in Kenya's wildlife parks.
6. the bigest city in Kenya is nairobi. (3)
   The biggest city in Kenya is Nairobi.
7. Nairobi are also the capital city (2)
   Nairobi is also the capital city.

© Carson Dellosa CD-3742 97

Name ______________________ **Proofreading**

Reading over your work to check it is called **proofreading**. Proofreading is important at school and also at home (like when you write a letter to a relative or friend).
When you proofread something you have written, check spelling, capital letters, punctuation marks, and grammar (to see that you have used words correctly).

Examples:

BEFORE PROOFREADING	AFTER PROOFREADING
Im leaving for schol.	**I'm** leaving for **school**.
I has no money for lunch.	I **have** no money for lunch.
In May 1989 I was born.	In May**,** 1989**,** I was born.

Dan wrote the paragraph below for social studies, but he forgot to proofread it! Read Dan's paragraph and draw a circle where something is incorrect or missing. Then rewrite the paragraph correctly below. There are 20 mistakes.

PIKE DISCOVERS A MOUNTAIN

Zebulon pike were an explorer who helped people learn more about north america In 1806 he left St. Louis missouri and headed west? He traveled up the arkansas river to the rocky mountains. In november 1906 he find a huge muntain. The mountain was named Pike's Peak and is now the most famous mountain in colorado. this discovery and Pike's other travels gave people important information about the southwestern part of Narth America.

Zebulon Pike was an explorer who helped people learn more about North America. In 1806 he left St. Louis, Missouri, and headed west. He traveled up the Arkansas River to the Rocky Mountains. In November, 1906 he found a huge mountain in Colorado. This discovery and Pike's other travels gave important information about the southwestern part of North America.

© Carson Dellosa CD-3742 98

Name ______________________ **Proofreading**

Bill has just written a fan letter. He forgot to proofread it. Find 20 mistakes in the letter. Then rewrite the letter correctly on the lines below.

March 9 1999

dea mr Hoops,

my mane is Bill and i am your biggest fan i love basketball and I really lo waching you play You is a great basketball player. Do you practice every day I herd that you use some of your money to hep kids go to college. You must be a really nise guy, too. could you please sent me a picture.

Your friend,

Bill

March 9, 1999

Dear Mr. Hoops,

My name is Bill and I am your biggest fan. I love basketball and really love watching you play. You are a great basketball player. Do you practice every day?

I heard that you use some of your money to help kids go to college. You must be a really nice guy, too. Could you please send me a picture?

Your friend,

Bill

© Carson-Dellosa CD-3742 99

! © CD-3742	. © CD-3742	? © CD-3742	a © CD-3742
adjective © CD-3742	Alyssa © CD-3742	am © CD-3742	apostrophe © CD-3742
are © CD-3742	article © CD-3742	books © CD-3742	brother © CD-3742
can’t © CD-3742	capital © CD-3742	clothes © CD-3742	colorful © CD-3742

command	comparison	compound	contraction
couldn’t	Dan	dark	desk
desks	didn’t	doctor’s	dog’s
excite	exciting	exclamation	gentle

glide 	hasn't 	haven't 	he
hold 	I 	irregular 	is
it 	lake 	letter 	listened
Lucy's 	mall 	Molly 	monkeys

neighbor © CD-3742	noun © CD-3742	office © CD-3742	paced © CD-3742
past tense © CD-3742	petals © CD-3742	planet © CD-3742	plant © CD-3742
player’s © CD-3742	plural © CD-3742	predicate © CD-3742	present © CD-3742
program © CD-3742	pronoun © CD-3742	proofread © CD-3742	proper © CD-3742

punctuation 	purple 	push 	question
ran 	Randy 	Roger 	rough
sentence 	she 	slipped 	slippery
smooth 	sofa 	statement 	study

ALLIES & ENEMIES

TEENAGE MUTANT NINJA

TURTLES

Letters and Collection Design by **Shawn Lee**
Series Edits by **Bobby Curnow**

Cover by **Dave Wilkins**
Collection Edits by **Justin Eisinger & Alonzo Simon**
Published by **Ted Adams**

Special thanks to Joan Hilty and Linda Lee for their invaluable assistance.

For international rights, contact **licensing@idwpublishing.com**

ISBN: 978-1-63140-613-3

19 18 17 16   1 2 3 4

IDW®
www.IDWPUBLISHING.com

Originally published as TEENAGE MUTANT NINJA TURTLES MICRO-SERIES issues #5 and 6 and TEENAGE MUTANT NINJA TURTLES VILLAINS MICRO-SERIES issues #1 and 7.

ALLIES & ENEMIES
TEENAGE MUTANT NINJA TURTLES

CASEY JONES

Written by **Mike Costa** and **Ben Epstein**
Art by **Mike Henderson**
Colors by **Ian Herring**

APRIL O'NEIL

Written by **Barbara Randall Kesel**
Art by **Marley Zarcone**
Colors by **Heather Breckel**

KRANG

Written by **Joshua Williamson**
Art by **Mike Henderson**
Colors by **Ian Herring**

BEBOP & ROCKSTEADY

Story by **Ben Bates & Dustin Weaver**
Script by **Dustin Weaver**
Art & Colors by **Ben Bates**

Art by **David Petersen**

EVERYTHING WAS SIMPLER ON THE HIGH-SCHOOL SQUAD.
CASEY JONES
I CALL SHENANIGANS.
NO WAY YOU SCORED TWO GOALS IN EIGHT MINUTES.

CAN *YOU* TYPE WITH *FIVE* FINGERS?
"YOU SHOULD GET BUSY IN THE LIBRARY," COACH TELLS ME.

CRAP.
CAN'T TELL HIM I'VE BEEN BUSY.

DON'T WORRY, SLUGGER.
YOU'LL GET 'EM NEXT TIME.
BUT NOT IN THE LIBRARY.

HEY, I NEVER SAID BASEBALL WAS MY SPORT.

MIND CALLING THE COPS? MY BUDDY LEFT HIS PHONE IN HIS OTHER SHELL.

WAY YOU THREW BACK THERE, I'D SAY YOUR SPORT IS "KNITTING."
NEXT TIME I'M PATROLLING WITH MICHELANGELO...

ARE YOU OKAY?
WE JUST GOT SAVED BY A GUY IN A HOCKEY MASK AND A GIANT TALKING TURTLE.

THIS IS WHAT HAPPENS WHEN WE GO SOUTH OF CANAL STREET.

WHEN I WAS NINE, MY OLD MAN DRAGGED ME OUT TO A FROZEN-OVER PARKING LOT ON THE COLDEST DAY OF WINTER.

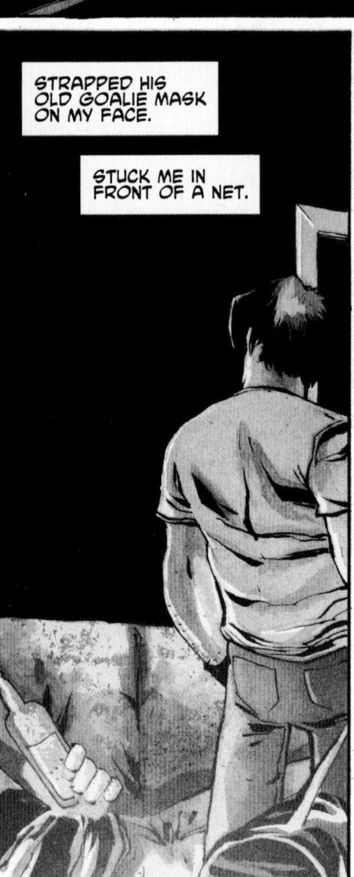
STRAPPED HIS OLD GOALIE MASK ON MY FACE.
STUCK ME IN FRONT OF A NET.

SHOT PUCKS AT ME TILL MY RIBS WERE BRUISED. MY FINGERS NEARLY FROZE OFF.

SAID THE COLD WOULD "TOUGHEN ME UP."
HE HAD A FLASK OF WHISKEY TO KEEP HIM WARM.

BUT HE DID TAKE ME FOR HOT CHOCOLATE AFTER.
AND THAT MASK STILL COMES IN HANDY.

ESPECIALLY ON LATE NIGHTS.
KNOCK KNOCK
WHOZAT...?
OPEN UP, ARNIE. IT'S BLAKE.
MIND IF WE COME IN?

HOW'S EVERYTHING? HOW'S YOUR BOY? CASEY, RIGHT?
HE'S OKAY.

SO YOU KNOW WHY I'M HERE. I HATE THIS, MAN. YOU'RE PUTTING ME IN A TOUGH SPOT.
WAY I REMEMBER IT, I GOT YOU OUT OF TOUGH SPOTS.
YOU DID...

...A LONG, LONG TIME AGO. BUT NOW YOU OWE ME A LOT OF MONEY.

AND I'M NOT THE ONE WHO GETS BEAT UP ANYMORE.

WHOA, HANG ON—JUST, JUST, HANG ON...

AHA!

THIS SHOULD COVER MY TAB, EASY.
I'M SORRY, BUT... THIS WON'T CUT IT. YOU STILL OWE FOUR LARGE.

I CAN GIVE YOU FORTY-EIGHT HOURS TO GET THE REST. FOR OLD TIMES' SAKE. BUT DON'T KEEP ME WAITING AGAIN.

SAY "HI" TO THAT BOY FOR ME. I REMEMBER HE HAD A WICKED SLAP-SHOT.

HEY MOM. YOU LOOK GOOD TODAY...
...WHAT DO YOU SAY WE BLOW OUT OF HERE? GET SOME DINNER?
LET ME *COUGH* GET MY COAT...

HOW WAS YOUR GAME?

I SCORED TWO GOALS AT THE END OF REGULATION. WE WON IN OVERTIME.

MY STRONG BOY.

YOUR HAIR IS TOO SHORT, THOUGH.

DID YOUR FATHER SEE YOU SCORE?

BUT THAT'LL HAVE TO WAIT.

C'MON! YOU CALL THAT *OFFENSE?*

WHAT'RE YOU *DOING?!* I DOUBLED DOWN ON YOU BUSTERS!

HEY LOOK! IT'S THE PLAYER VOTED "MOST LIKELY TO BUST HIS HEAD OPEN!"

THANKS FOR COMING.
SURE. WHAT'S UP? WE'RE NOT SET TO PATROL FOR A WEEK.

NOT PATROL. MORE OF A STAKEOUT.
OH YEAH? WHO ARE WE PEEPING? PUNKS? PROWLERS? PUSHERS? PILL-POPPERS?

I JUST WANNA KEEP AN EYE ON SOME GUYS WHO NEED AN EYE KEPT ON 'EM. ALL RIGHT?

...SURE. NO PROBLEM.

I THINK THIS PLACE SMELLS.

AND MY BUDDIES HANG OUT IN THE SEWERS.

SO THIS DIVE'S A GOOD FIT FOR SUCKERS BLAKE CAN PLAY, LIKE THIS GUY...

...AND DRUNKS LIKE MY OLD MAN.

I KNOW IT'S NOT EASY. YOUR FATHER'S NOT STRONG, LIKE YOU.
WHATEVER. HE'S A STUPID DRUNK—

CASEY ARNOLD JONES!

SORRY.
REMEMBER. HE'S LOSING ME, JUST LIKE YOU ARE.

AND IF HE ACTS TOUGH, IT'S JUST BECAUSE HE'S SCARED.
YOU'LL NEED TO TAKE CARE OF HIM WHEN I'M GONE.

YOU'RE GONNA BE FINE, MOM.
CASEY. WHEN I'M GONE, YOU NEED TO TAKE CARE OF HIM.

"PROMISE ME."
—STARTED WITH SUCH PROMISE BUT THEN, AFTER A DISASTROUS FINAL QUARTER—

CASEY... WHY'RE WE WATCHING THESE GUYS WATCH A GAME?
I'VE BEEN LESS BORED WATCHING SPLINTER MEDITATE—
SHH!

I'M SORRY, MATTHEW, BUT THAT GAME DID NOT GO YOUR WAY.
MR. ANDERS-BLAKE—I'M GOOD FOR IT. I SWEAR. LOOK, YOU KNOW ME...
CENZO. CARLO...
LET'S ALL TAKE A WALK.

LET'S GO.

I'M SORRY, MATTHEW. THIS IS NO FUN FOR ME.

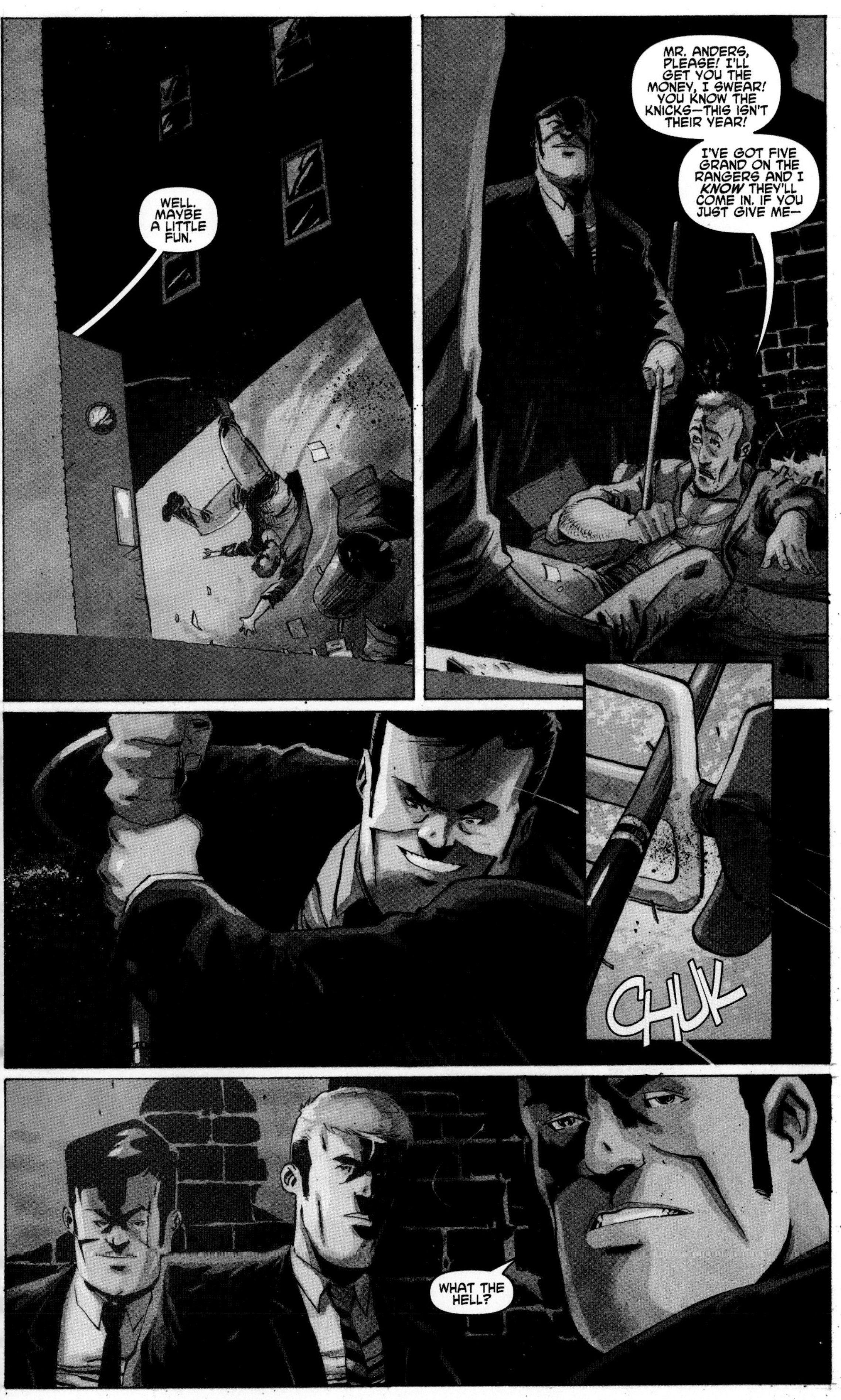

WELL. MAYBE A LITTLE FUN.

MR. ANDERS, PLEASE! I'LL GET YOU THE MONEY, I SWEAR! YOU KNOW THE KNICKS—THIS ISN'T THEIR YEAR!

I'VE GOT FIVE GRAND ON THE RANGERS AND I *KNOW* THEY'LL COME IN. IF YOU JUST GIVE ME—

CHUK

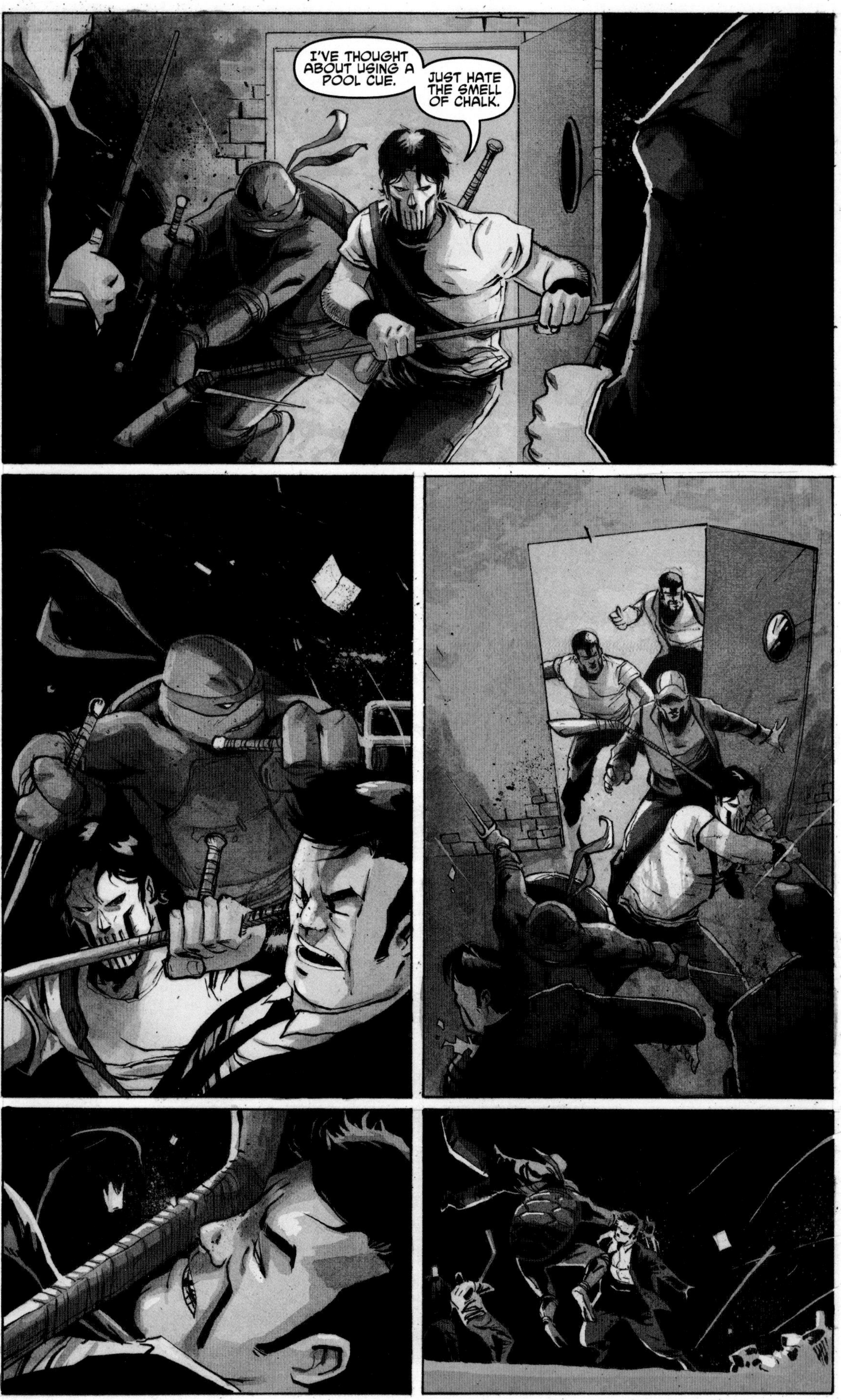

I'VE THOUGHT ABOUT USING A POOL CUE.
JUST HATE THE SMELL OF CHALK.

ARG!

MATTHEW'S PAID UP.
SURE... YOU GOT IT... ALL PAID UP...

YOU COME AFTER HIM, AND A LOT WORSE THINGS THAN *THIS* WILL HAPPEN TO *YOU.*
AND ARNOLD JONES IS PAID UP TOO. HE'S OFF-LIMITS.
...JONES...?

JONES IS OFF-LIMITS.

RAPH? YOU GOOD?

I'M GOOD.

GAMBLING'S A BAD HABIT.
STOP DOING IT.

HEY MAN, SEEMED LIKE THINGS GOT PRETTY INTENSE.
HAPPY TO HELP, BUT WHAT WERE WE DOING THERE?
KEEPIN' A PROMISE.

STRONG PEOPLE DON'T HAVE TO REMIND PEOPLE THEY'RE STRONG. THEY JUST ARE.
LIKE YOU, CASEY.
LIKE YOU TOO, MOM.

...MAYBE.

MEANT TO COME EARLIER, BUT... I GOT...

...HELD UP.
IT'S ALL RIGHT, ARNIE. I'M HERE.

I'M HERE.

WHERE THE HELL WERE YOU, MUTT?
NOWHERE.
IS THAT SASS? YOU GOT A SMART MOUTH, DON'T YOU, YOU PIECE OF CRAP.
DAD, JUST LET ME GO TO BED.
YOU THINK YOU'RE SOME TOUGH GUY?

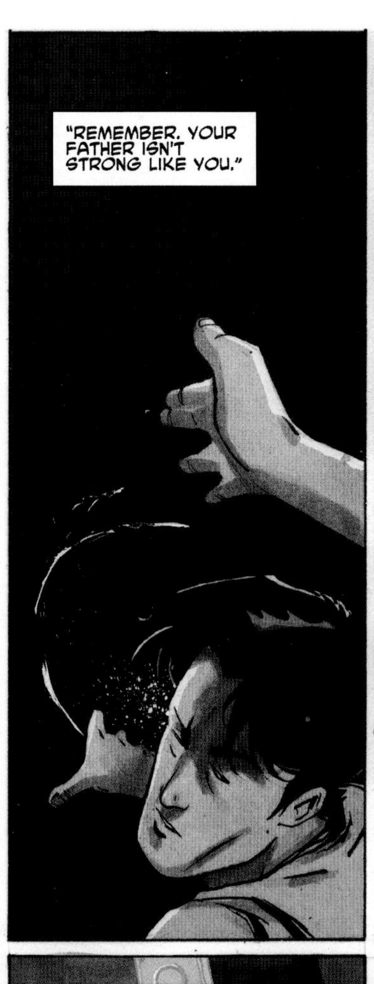
"REMEMBER, YOUR FATHER ISN'T STRONG LIKE YOU."

AND PART OF THE WAY YOU HAVE TO TAKE CARE OF HIM IS NOT LETTING HIM SEE THAT.

"PROMISE ME YOU'LL LET HIM FEEL STRONG."

I'M TRYING TO KEEP MY PROMISE, MOM...
...BUT I DON'T KNOW HOW MUCH LONGER I CAN KEEP GOING LIKE THIS.
THE SECOND TIME AROUND 2 SHOPS

WHOA!
CASEY!

WHAT HAPPENED?! RAPH SAID YOU GUYS DIDN'T GET HURT!
MY DAD... DIDN'T LIKE MY "SMART MOUTH."
IT'S FINE.
OPEN

DUDE... CASEY... ARE YOU OKAY?
'COURSE I AM... I CAN TAKE IT... NO PROBLEM...

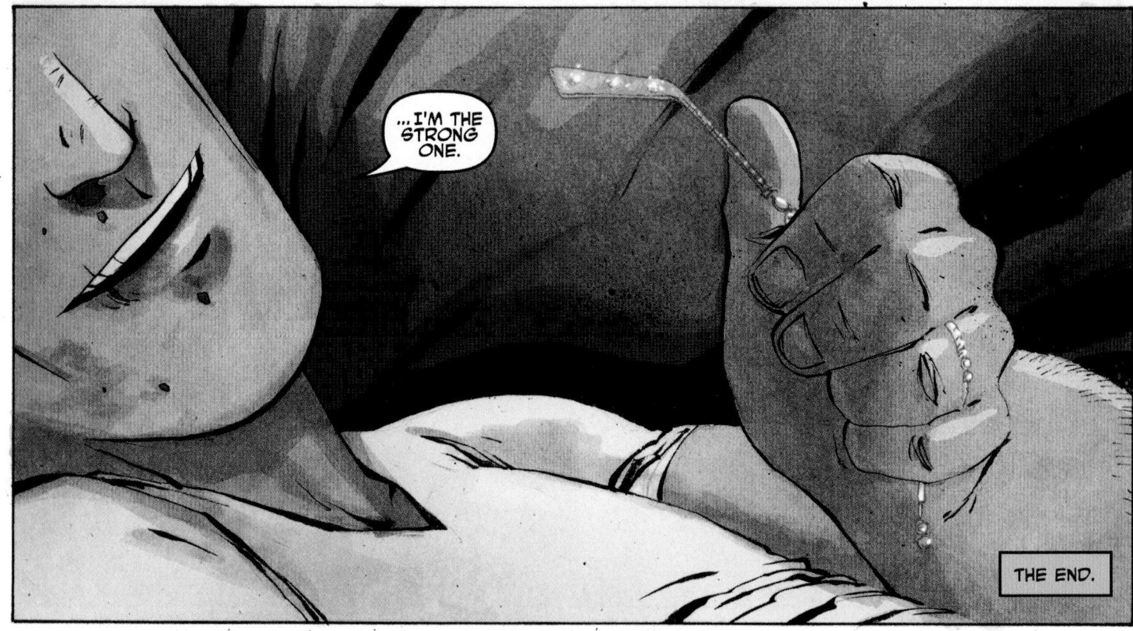
...I'M THE STRONG ONE.
THE END.

Art by **Mike Henderson**

Art by **David Petersen**

APRIL
NOOOOO!
NONONONO!
AHH!
NONONONONO...
...NO MORE PIZZA AT BEDTIME.
STRANGE DREAM.
LIKE MY REALITY ISN'T.

YEAH, IT'S STRANGE, ALL RIGHT...
HEY, APRIL—YOU GOT A HULA GIRL TO GO WITH THAT PALM TREE?
SHE'D TAKE ONE SNIFF AND RUN AWAY IN FEAR!
MY VAN'S SMELLED PRETTY RIPE SINCE I MET YOU GUYS...
KLK KLK KLK KLK
THAT'S TURTLE POWER!
MAYBE PEOPLE WOULDN'T SHY AWAY FROM THE WEIRD SO MUCH IF THEY KNEW HOW MUCH OF OUR NATURAL WORLD IS TRULY BIZARRE.
IT'S NOT ONE I'D BRAG ABOUT.
SORRY, APRIL. MY BROTHERS AREN'T EXACTLY MASTERS OF PERSONAL HYGIENE.
KLK KLK KLK
ANY BIOLOGIST KNOWS THAT A MICROSCOPE PROVES OUR WORLD IS FILLED WITH STRANGE BEINGS AND CRAZY SCI-FI ENVIRONMENTS.
WHEN YOU CHANGE THE SCALE, YOUR PERCEPTION OF "NORMAL" ADJUSTS.
LIKE YOU DON'T SMELL JUST THE SAME AS THE REST OF US, DONNIE!
SO I'M USED TO THE WEIRD.
HEY, DONNIE, WHY DON'TCHA KNOCK IT OFF WITH THE CLICKING, WILLYA?
YOU'RE MAKING MY BRAIN HURT!
KLK KLK KLK KLK
SORRY. IT HELPS ME CLEAR MY HEAD.
LOOK, GUYS, I KNOW YOU DON'T WANT TO THINK ABOUT IT, BUT WE'RE TOO VULNERABLE LIVING ABOVE GROUND AT APRIL'S SHOP. NOTHING'S STOPPING STOCKMAN FROM BUILDING ANOTHER TURTLE TRACKER AND FINDING THE SHOP.
IT IS TAKING A LITTLE LONGER...

...TO GET OVER THE NOVELTY OF HAVING IT TALK TO ME.
NOT THE TURTLE TRACKER HUNT AGAIN! THAT THING GOT DESTROYED!*
*See TMNT MICRO-SERIES: DONATELLO.
ONE WAS DESTROYED.
YEAH. I HAVE TALKING HUMANOID TURTLES IN MY VAN.
LET IT GO, DONNIE. DON'T BORROW TROUBLE.
THEY'RE THE ONES IN TROUBLE! IF THEY COME A'TRACKIN', THEY'LL GET A SMACKIN'!
NINJA STYLE!
NINJA STYLE IS SUBTLE AND INVISIBLE.
THEIR VERBALIZATION ALONE IS A BIOLOGICAL ANOMALY.
THE NINJA THING IS ANOTHER LEVEL OF WEIRDNESS ALTOGETHER.
IF I COULD JUST ANALYZE ITS CIRCUITRY TO DETERMINE—
ENGLISH, DUDE!
MY TURTLES ARE A WALKING, TALKING, SUCCESSFUL EXPERIMENT IN BIOCHEMICAL ENGINEERING.
IF I CAN PLAY WITH IT, IT'LL BE EASY-PEASY TO MAKE IT NOT WORK!
IS THAT ENGLISH ENOUGH?
OR MAYBE JUST AN ACCIDENTAL MIRACLE.

WE'RE TAUGHT, AS SCIENTISTS, TO MAINTAIN A DISPASSIONATE OBSERVER ROLE.
IT'S HOW I HANDLE STRESS—OBJECTIFY AND ANALYZE. USE SCIENCE TO SHIELD MY HEART.
BUT I CAN'T DO THAT WITH THE TURTLES. I FEEL TOO PROTECTIVE OF THEM NOW.
AFTER ALL, I *NAMED* THEM.
THE BIOLOGIST IN ME IS FASCINATED. HOW MANY VARIABLES WERE INVOLVED? THE LENGTH OF EXPOSURE TO A MUTAGENIC AGENT, INTERFERENCE FROM THE FOOT NINJA, CONTAMINATION OF THE ALLEY ENVIRONMENT...
...THE FRIEND IN ME WONDERS...
...BECOMING LUCID... AWARE... MORE HUMAN, DID IT *HURT* THEM?
NOW MY TURTLES LIVE LIKE FUGITIVES.
WE DID THAT—GOOD OL' STOCKGEN.
STOCKGEN RESEARCH INC.
ENGINEERING A FUTURE STOCKED WITH SCIENTIFIC INNOVATI
I USED TO BELIEVE IN THE PURITY OF SCIENCE.
THE PROCESS OF EXPERIMENTATION AND REPLICATION YIELDING RELIABLE RESULTS. ADDING TO THE WEALTH OF HUMAN KNOWLEDGE.
STUDYING THE BEAUTIFUL MYSTERIES OF REALITY.
BUT THAT'S CRAP.
CIE
NOVAT

I'M FINDING THAT CORPORATE SCIENCE IS JUST AS CORRUPT AS ANY OTHER BIG BUSINESS.
IF THEY CAN TRACK THE TURTLES DOWN, THEY'LL PROBABLY VIVISECT THEM, SELL WHAT THEY LEARN, AND JUSTIFY IT AS SCIENCE.
CAFE
LAB
I CAN'T LET THAT HAPPEN.
I WANT TO LEAP INTO ACTION AND HELP!
BUT THAT'S MY HEART LEAPING, NOT MY HEAD. I NEED A PLAN.
I ALREADY KNOW STOCKGEN'S GOT A SCIENTIFIC DARK ALLEY—THE TURTLES ARE PROOF.
WHAT'S MISSING IS *EVIDENCE*.
WHICH HAS TO BE *HERE* SOMEWHERE.
HOW CAN I FIND IT? I'M NO NINJA...
...AND NOT, DESPITE CASEY'S HELP, REALLY A FIGHTER...
CLEARANCE
STOCKGEN
CAFE
...BUT I COULD...
...BE A *SPY*.

SO THIS IS THE T-TRACKING UNIT?
HOW EXACTLY DOES IT DETECT THE TERRAPI—
G-GOOD MORNING, APRIL!
STOCKGEN RESEARCH INC.
ENGINEERING A FUTUR STOCKED WITH SCIENTIFIC INNOVATIO
TERRAPIN? TURTLE?
THAT'S DONATELLO'S TRACKER?
GOT A NEW TV REMOTE THERE, CHET?
UH...

THERE'S GOT TO BE SOMETHING...
...SOMETHING SIMPLE!
NONE OF MY BUSINESS, I'M SURE.
ANYWAY, DO YOU HAVE THE NUTRIENT SCHEDULE FOR THE–
FLUID MECHANICS PLUS PSYCHOLOGY EQUALS...
WHUPS!
...PINBALL!
POOR CHET...
...LOOK WHAT I MADE YOU DO!
KRZIIII

STOCKGEN
EXPERIMENT SERIES 2051 - 2076
FAILURE
STOCKGEN
EXPERIMENT SERIES 2051 - 2077
FAILURE
STOCKGEN
EXPERIMENT SERIES 2051 - 2078
FAILURE

BWRRRRRRRRRRR
...IS A *BIG* SUCCESS.

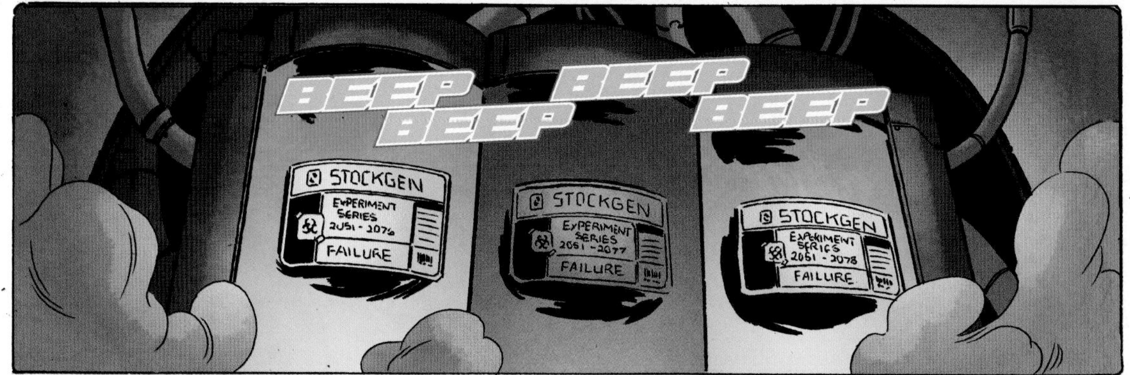
BEEP
BEEP
BEEP
BEEP
STOCKGEN
EXPERIMENT SERIES 2051 - 2076
FAILURE
STOCKGEN
EXPERIMENT SERIES 2051 - 2077
FAILURE
STOCKGEN
EXPERIMENT SERIES 2051 - 2078
FAILURE

STOCKGEN
EXPERIMENT SERIES
2051 - 2078
FAILURE

I– I– HOW C-COULD...?
I'M SURE YOU DIDN'T MEAN FOR THAT TO HAPPEN.
B-BUT I–
–I D-DIDN'T!
NO ONE'S BLAMING YOU.
CAN I HELP YOU CLEAN UP?
EVERYBODY OUT! YOU CAN COME BACK AFTER WE GIVE THE ALL CLEAR.

—NOT SURE IF THEY WERE PLANNING TO USE IT SOON, BUT FOR NOW, IT'S SAFELY STASHED AND YOU CAN HAVE IT IN YOUR HANDS BY TOMORROW!
I TOLD YOU WE NEEDED TO PAY ATTENTION TO THAT TURTLE TRACKER TECH!
OKAY, DONNIE, YOU'RE NOT AS CRAZY AS WE THOUGHT!
STOCKGEN

YOU DID GOOD, APRIL!
ABSOLUTELY, APRIL, BUT YOU SHOULDN'T TAKE ANY MORE BIG RISKS ON OUR BEHALF.
YOU REALLY THINK YOU GUYS ARE THE ONLY ONES WHO SHOULD TAKE RISKS?
NO, BUT–
DON'T YOU WANT TO GET YOUR HANDS ON THAT TRACKER?
IF I GET CAUGHT, I JUST SAY I WAS CURIOUS ABOUT THE DAMAGE AND WHOOPS! I USED THE WRONG I.D!
O... KAY. JUST BE CAREFUL.

NOTHING TO SEE HERE...
...JUST A JOGGER, PAY NO ATTENTION.
NOBODY SPECIAL.
MOVE ALONG, MOVE ALONG. JUST AN ORDINARY COWORKER BACK TO CHECK ON THE DAMAGE.
YOU SEE ME EVERY DAY. DON'T BOTHER LOOKING AT...
...THAT?
—HOW UNHAPPY GENERAL KRANG WILL BE IF THE BIOLOGICAL AREAS ARE NOT RESECURED SOON.
HOLD ON! THAT GUY IS SOLID STONE!
EVERYTHING SEEMS F-FINE. IT WAS JUST A SHORT-CIRCUIT.
AND CHET'S NOT SURPRISED?
I THOUGHT THE TURTLE TRACKER WAS SOMETHING—
THERE'S MUCH BIGGER SECRETS HERE!

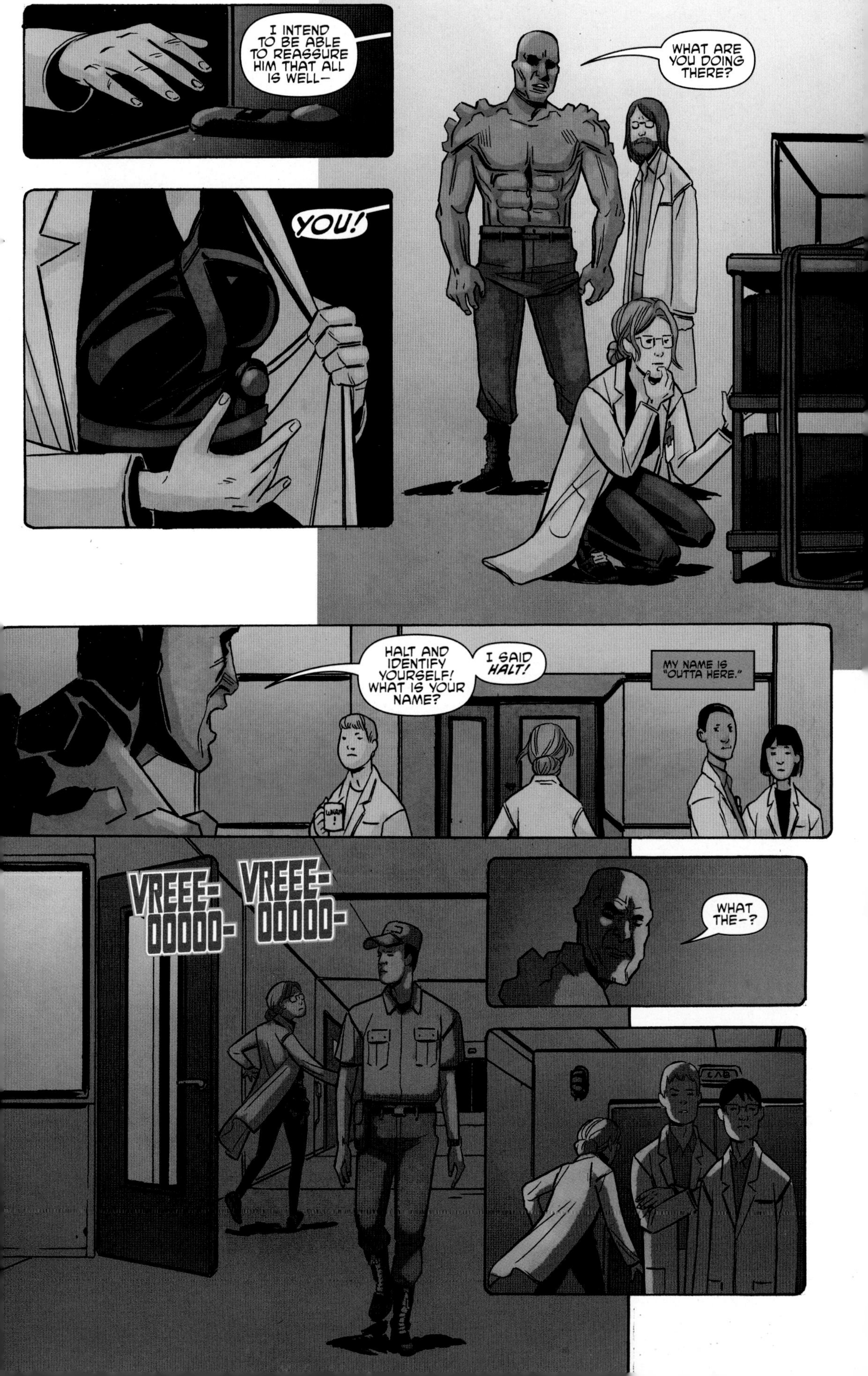

HALT AND IDENTIFY YOURSELF! WHAT IS YOUR NAME?

I SAID *HALT!*

MY NAME IS "OUTTA HERE."

VREEE-OOOOO- VREEE-OOOOO-

WHAT THE–?

I REVISE MY EARLIER ASSESSMENT.
MY NAME IS NOW "TOTALLY SCREWED."
VREEE-OOOOO-VREEE-OOOOO-VREEE
NO STONE GUY...
...MAYBE HE THINKS I BOLTED FOR THE EXIT?
WHERE AM I?
WHAT IS THIS?
GENETIC MANIPULATION.
THE TURTLES WERE ONLY THE BEGINNING...

...AND FROM THE LOOKS OF THE DAMAGE...
<GEN
IMENT
IES
2077
ILURE
...SOMEBODY ELSE GOT TIRED OF BEING AN EXPERIMENT.
I CAN'T IGNORE WHAT I'M SEEING HERE.
I TOLD YOU TO HALT!
KRAK

VREEE-OOOOO-VREEE-OOOOO-VREEE
THIS IS FRIGHTENINGLY FAMILIAR...
...ONLY I'M NOT DREAMING THIS TIME.
THERE'S NO WAY OUT EXCEPT THROUGH HIM.
THINK, APRIL. YOU MAY NOT HAVE A SHELL, BUT YOU HAVE A BRAIN.
OBJECTIFY AND ANALYZE.
KA-CHNKK
AHH!
PSSSSHH
THANKS FOR THE SELF-DEFENSE LESSONS, CASEY—
LET'S HOPE I ACE MY FINAL!

KLANGK
KREESH
IT'S THE OLDEST RELATIONSHIP IN THE NATURAL WORLD, RIGHT?
HE'S THE PREDATOR, I'M THE PREY.
I AM WAY OUTMATCHED.
ADRENALINE IS PRETTY COOL STUFF. CLEARS YOUR HEAD.
LETS YOUR BODY DO WHAT IT NEEDS TO DO IN THAT "FIGHT OR FLIGHT" MOMENT.
SO I SHOULD BE TERRIFIED.
AND I AM. MY BRAIN JUST DOESN'T KNOW IT YET.

VREEE-OOOOO-
VREEE-OOOOO-
VREEE-

TOO BAD IT DOESN'T LAST FOREVER.

PRETTY SOON I'M GONNA CRASH.

BEFORE THAT HAPPENS, I NEED TO...

...*ESCAPE*.

WHAT—?

GRAAAUGH!
THOK
CRASH
EE-OOOOO-VREEE-OOOOO-VREEE-OOOOO-VR

VREEE-OOOOO-VREEE-OOOOO-
THERE! FOLLOW ME!
ALL CLEAR?
THANK GOD. ALL CLEAR.
AT LEAST FOR NOW.
EE-OOOOO-VREEE-OOOOO-VREEE-
YOU! FREEZE!

I HAVE NO PLAN FOR GETTING OUT THE DOOR, BUT IT DOESN'T MATTER. IT'S ABANDONED.
WHATEVER THAT ROCKY GUY WAS YELLING ABOUT, THEY'RE ALL BUSY CHASING IT.
SO I'M OUT WITH THE TRACKER AND MORE QUESTIONS THAN ANSWERS.
TYPICAL SCIENTIFIC SCENARIO.
IT *IS* CREEPY BEING OUT HERE THIS LATE...
WELCOME TO STOCKGEN
BUT I'M NOT AFRAID OF ANYTHING ANYMORE.
THMPP
NOT AFTER *THAT.*
THMMMP
JUST SICK AND SAD KNOWING WHAT'S *REALLY* GOING ON IN THERE.
WHANNNG

THAT'S WHAT HAPPENS WHEN SCIENCE GOES BAD.
WHO KNOWS WHAT OTHER BEINGS THEY MIGHT TORTURE INTO EXISTENCE?
WHAT I *DO* KNOW IS WHO'S GOING TO BE THERE TO STOP THEM.
FOUR TALKING HUMANOID TURTLES...
...AND A HOCKEY PLAYER WITH ISSUES...
...AND *ME.*
THE END.

Art by **Marley Zarcone**

Art by Tyler Walpole

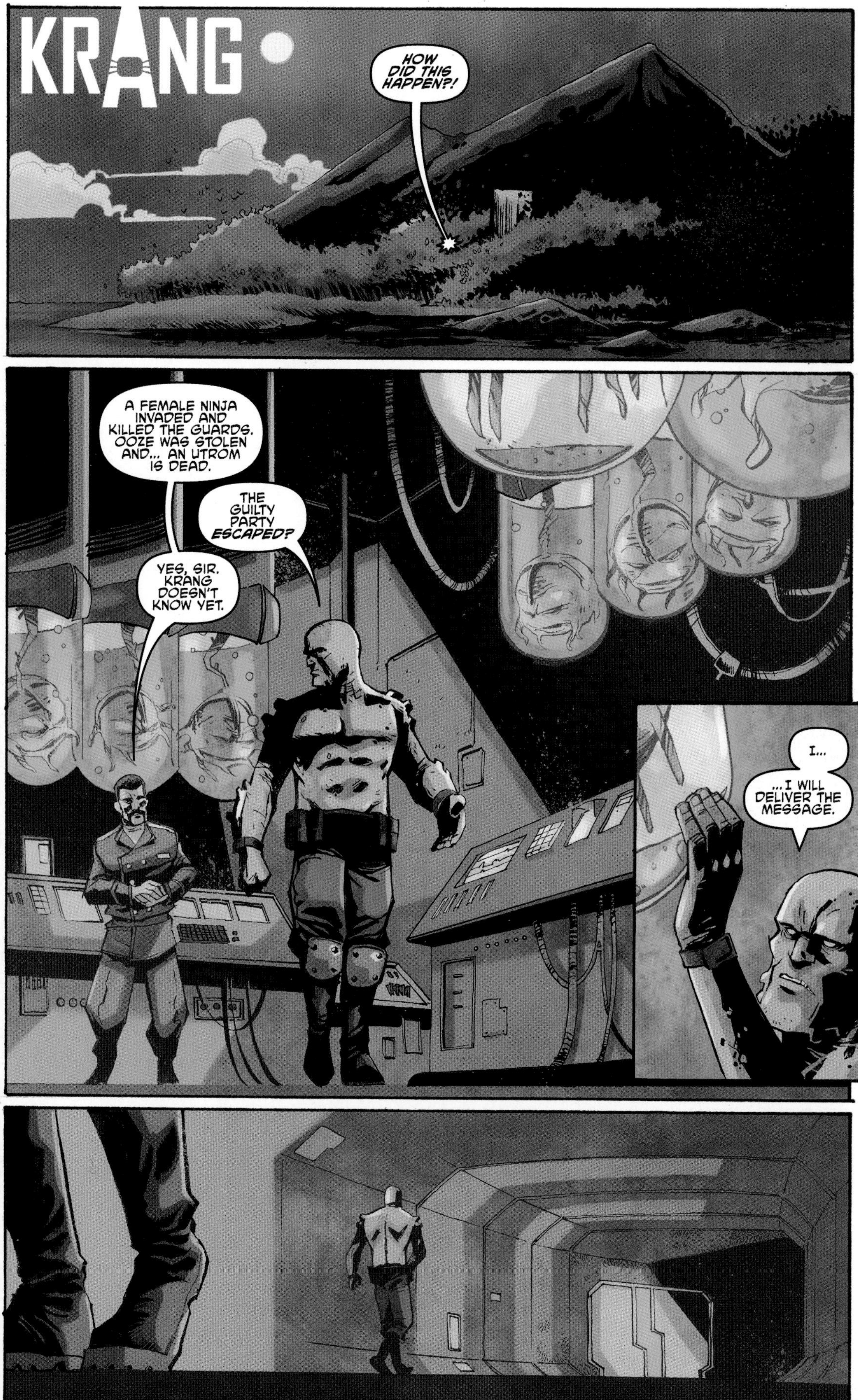

A FEMALE NINJA INVADED AND KILLED THE GUARDS. OOZE WAS STOLEN AND... AN UTROM IS DEAD.

THE GUILTY PARTY *ESCAPED?*

YES, SIR. KRANG DOESN'T KNOW YET.

I...

...I WILL DELIVER THE MESSAGE.

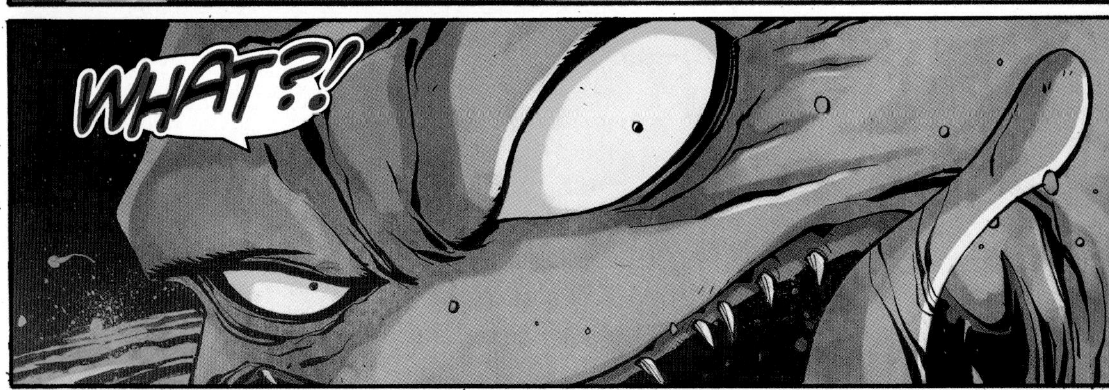
GENERAL?
I GAVE ORDERS THAT I WAS NOT TO BE DISTURBED!
YES, SIR, BUT... ONE OF THE UTROMS HAS DIED IN STASIS.
THE SECURITY FOOTAGE SUGGESTS THAT IT WAS... A FEMALE NINJA OF SOME KIND.
WHAT?!
WE WERE LETTING YOU RECUPERATE FROM YOUR FIGHT WITH THE—
STAND BACK!
YOU DO NOT ASSIST ME UNLESS ORDERED!
I DON'T NEED YOUR HELP!
THE SOLDIER IS UPSET, BUT I DON'T SEE TERROR IN HIS EYES. HE HAS FORGOTTEN HIS PLACE.

HAVE I GROWN SOFT? HAVE MY SETBACKS AT THE HANDS OF THOSE BLASTED NEUTRINOS CHANGED THE WAY MY FORCES LOOK AT ME?
DO THEY SEE ME AS WEAK?
I WAS NOT ALWAYS AS POWERFUL AS I AM NOW.
PLANET UTROMINON.
BRING ME MY WALKER, YOU WORTHLESS TOADS!
IN MY YOUTH I WAS MORE...
...DEPENDENT.
I DEMAND YOU BRING MY MEAL TO ME. AND BRING ME A DIFFERENT SCREEN! I'M BORED WITH THESE!
YES, KRANG.
THAT'S MASTER KRANG!
KRANG!
ARE YOUR OWN TENTACLES BROKEN? ARE YOU TOO BUSY WITH YOUR LITTLE GAMES TO DO ANYTHING FOR YOURSELF?
FATHER, I-I-I MERELY THOUGHT THAT I NEEDED TO SHOW THEM THEIR PLACE.
THAT I COULD BE AS GREAT A RULER AND LEADER AS YOU.

THE COUNCIL IS READY TO DISCUSS THE OFFENSIVE AGAINST TRAXUS, SIR.

GOOD. FOLLOW ME.

FATHER... CAN I JOIN YOU?

WHY ON UTROMINON WOULD I WANT *YOU* THERE?

MY FATHER'S ANCIENT ENEMY, TRAXUS, HAD BEEN IMPRISONED IN THE PENITENTIARY ON MORBUS, A PLANET WITH A HOSTILE ENVIRONMENT, WHERE THE UTROM HIGH COUNCIL'S MOST DANGEROUS POLITICAL PRISONERS WERE HELD.

NOW HE HAD OVERTHROWN THE PRISON GUARDS AND ASSEMBLED AN ARMY OF MEN WHO HATED MY FATHER AS MUCH AS HE DID... AND THEY WERE PLOTTING THE DEMISE OF THE UTROM EMPIRE.

MY FATHER AND THE COUNCIL PLANNED AN ATTACK TO SQUASH THE REBELLION.
IT WILL BE A SUICIDE MISSION!
ONLY IF WE DO WHAT THEY EXPECT-- A DIRECT ATTACK ON THE PENITENTIARY. BUT LANDING IN THE SWAMP TO THE NORTH... THAT WILL ALLOW US TO MOVE IN UNDETECTED AND ATTACK AT THE MOST ADVANTAGEOUS TIME.
THE SWAMP IS A HELLHOLE... THEY WON'T EXPECT US TO LAND *THERE.*

TRAXUS WILL *PAY.*
IT WAS A MISSION CHARGED TO THE BEST WARRIORS UTROMINON HAD TO OFFER.

IF I WAS EVER GOING TO PROVE MY WORTH TO MY FATHER...
...NOW WAS THE TIME.
ZZZOOWOSSH
HOPE YOU BOYS ARE READY!
MORBUS IS ONE OF THE MOST HOSTILE BATTLEGROUNDS YOU'LL EVER KNOW.
AND IT'LL BE EVEN MORE DEADLY UNDER TRAXUS' COMMAND.
BUT NO MANGY BUNCH OF PRISONERS CAN TAKE ON UTROMINON'S BEST!

I KNEW THE RISK OF STOWING AWAY—BUT THE SENSE OF DANGER WAS EXHILARATING AFTER A LIFETIME OF SAFETY AND COMFORT.

I WOULD KNOW *BATTLE*. I WOULD *DOMINATE*.
WWHOOSSSHH

I WOULD RETURN HOME AS A *HERO*.

FOR ONCE, MY FATHER WOULD BE *PROUD* OF ME.

MEN, AFTER OUR POSITION IS *SECURE*, YOU'LL HEAD FOR HIGH GROUND. I WANT TO KNOW EXACTLY WHAT IS BETWEEN US AND THE PENITENTIARY.
TRAXUS WON'T KNOW WHAT HIT HIM.

KOOM
COMMANDER!
DON'T MOVE! THEY'VE MINED THE AREA!
W-WHAT'S THAT NOISE?
VRRMMMM
AH, ANOTHER OF QUANIN'S CLASSIC "SNEAK" ATTACKS.
VRRMMMM
THOSE JUST NEVER GET OLD, DO THEY?
ATTACK!
KST KST KST KST KST KST KST KST KST KST KST
TRAXUS KNEW MY FATHER'S TACTICS TOO WELL.
SO HE HAD *PREPARED* THE AREA... AND WAITED TO SHOOT US LIKE CHAINED BEASTS.
I HAD NEVER EVEN IMAGINED SUCH DESTRUCTION.

BOOM
THIS WAS THE FINEST QUANIN COULD SEND?
UGGH...
MY OLD ENEMY HAS LOST HIS *FIRE.*
SPLAT
DESTROYING HIM IS GOING TO BE EASIER THAN I THOUGHT.
LEAVE THEM TO *BURN*. WE'LL RETURN WHEN THE STENCH HAS BEEN BLOWN AWAY BY THE WIND.

WHETHER IT WAS BY LUCK OR FATE THAT I MADE IT OUT OF THE ATTACK ALIVE, I DIDN'T *CARE*. THERE WERE MORE PRESSING ISSUES AT HAND...
...THE SWAMPS OF MORBUS WERE INFAMOUSLY DANGEROUS. PLANTS, ANIMALS AND TERRAIN—ALL *DEADLY*.
THE ACID RAIN ALONE WAS STRONG ENOUGH TO KILL.
IF I DIDN'T MOVE QUICKLY, I WOULD DIE...
...AND I WOULD DIE UNDISCOVERED. ALONE.
NEVER TO LEAD MY PEOPLE.

MY FATHER WAS RIGHT.
KKSHHSSS
ARGH!

I HAD MADE MYSELF WORTHLESS.
DESTINED TO DIE LIKE PREY.

GET BACK, VILE CREATURE!

THK

HISS

BUT THEN SOMETHING MIRACULOUS HAPPENED.

I LIVED.
AND AS THE HOURS STRETCHED INTO DAYS I REALIZED...

...I WAS STRONGER THAN I KNEW.
I WAS THE ONLY UTROM TO LIVE THROUGH TRAXUS' ATTACK, AND I WAS STILL ALIVE ON THIS DEADLY PLANET. I WAS A SURVIVOR.

I WOULD PROVE WHAT I WAS CAPABLE OF.

...AND THE NEW KRANG COULD TAKE CARE OF HIMSELF.

BUT SIMPLY SURVIVING WASN'T ENOUGH. I NEEDED TO FINISH THE MISSION.

I WOULD *NOT* QUIT.

EVERYONE, INCLUDING MY FATHER, DOUBTED MY WORTH.

NO LONGER WERE MY DAYS WASTED WITH TOYS AND PAMPERING.

THE ***HELPLESS KRANG*** WAS GONE...

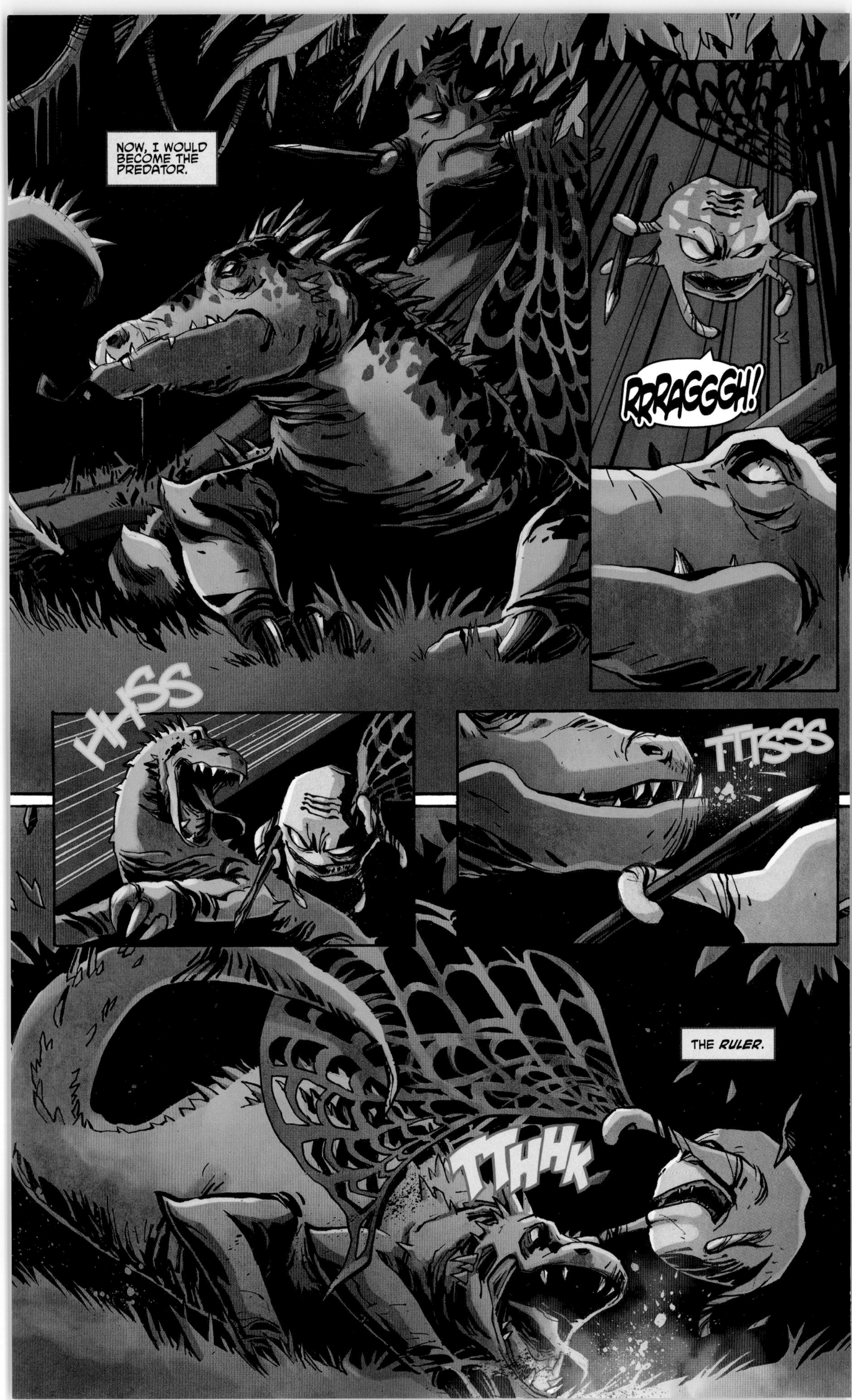
NOW, I WOULD BECOME THE PREDATOR.
RRRAGGGH!
HISS
TTTSSS
THE RULER.
TTHHK

HHHSSS
HHSSSS

FROM NOW ON...

...ANY CHALLENGER WOULD *DIE* AT MY HANDS...

...*RETREAT* IN AN INSTANT, OR BECOME...

...*MINE TO RULE*.

THIS CURSED PLANET WOULD BE *CONQUERED*.

MY FATHER HAD TRIED TO WIN WITH

TRAXUS!

SIR, LET TRAGG AND I–

NO, GRANITOR. I CAN TAKE ON THIS PATHETIC LITTLE UTROM MYSELF.

THEN I'LL SEND HIS LIFELESS BODY BACK TO HIS FATHER SO QUANIN CAN ADD TO HIS LONG LIST OF *FAILURES*.

HSSS

RRRAAAHHH!

AAAHHH!

DIE! DIE!

UK.

WHA-WHAT ARE YOU DOING?

CHUK

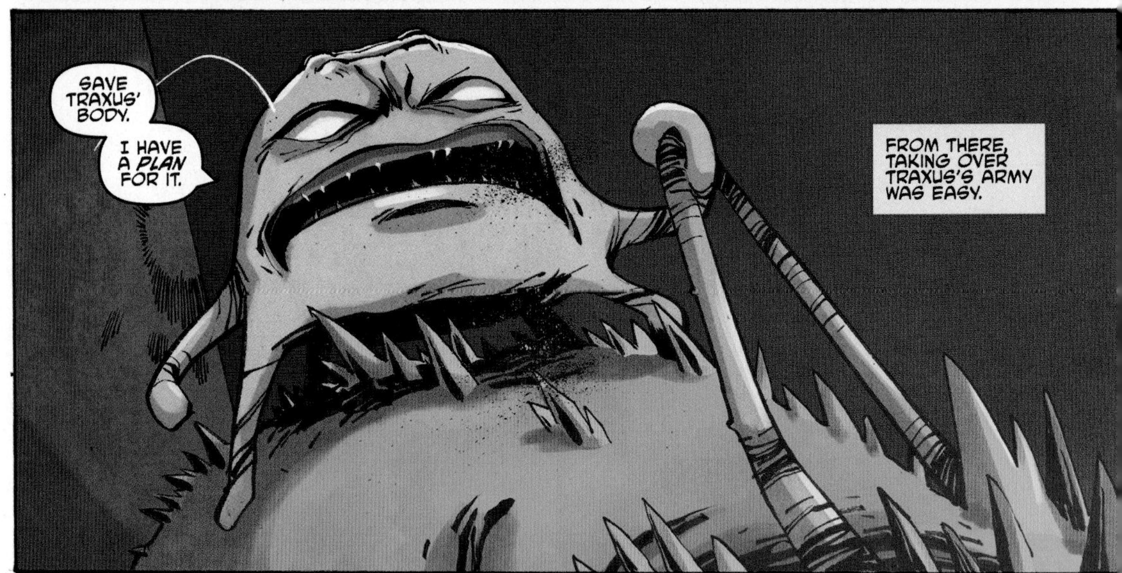

WITH TRAGG AND GRANITOR'S HELP, MANY OF TRAXUS'S MEN SAW THAT I WAS THE FUTURE.
THAT I WAS THEIR TRUE LEADER. AND THEY PLEDGED THEIR LIVES TO ME.
INSTEAD OF RETURNING THE PRISONERS TO THE CELLS, I OFFERED THEM A CHANCE TO WORK FOR ME.
SOME TOOK THE OFFER...
...SOME DIDN'T.
BY THE TIME MY FATHER ARRIVED...
...ALL OF MORBUS WAS MINE.
I HAVE A HARD TIME BELIEVING THAT KRANG COULD EVER—

GREETINGS, EMPEROR QUANIN.
MY ARMY IS AT YOUR DISPOSAL.
IT IS GOOD TO SEE YOU... MY SON.
THAT WAS THE FIRST TIME MY FATHER HAD CALLED ME HIS SON IN AGES. FINALLY, HE LOOKED UPON ME AS I DESERVED...

...WITH RESPECT.

PLEASE FORGIVE ME, GENERAL KRANG.
I'LL UNDERSTAND ANY PUNISHMENT YOU GIVE ME, SIR.

DON'T BURDEN YOURSELF WITH THOSE KINDS OF THOUGHTS, SOLDIER.
COME, COME...

...GO AHEAD AND HELP ME.
I GIVE YOU PERMISSION. DON'T MAKE ME ORDER YOU.

YES, GENERAL.

AND NO ONE...
...NEUTRINO, NINJA OR MUTANT...
...WILL STAND IN MY WAY.
THE END.

Art by Mike Henderson

Art by **Tyler Walpole**

PUNCH!

YOU CAN'T DO THIS TO— UGH!

IT WAS AN ACCIDENT!

WE GOT NOTHING!
NO GANG, NO POWER, WE AIN'T EVEN GOT NO FREAKIN' FOOD!
HEY, IT'S COOL. WHADDYA SAY WE GO SCORE SOME CASH? WE'LL STICK UP SOME CHUMP, OR JACK THAT CASH MACHINE LIKE WE WAS TALKING A—
BASH
NO! I'M *SICK* OF THIS!
WE GOTTA FIND *SOME* WAY OF GETTING OUT OF THIS HOLE WE'RE IN. WE CAN'T SCREW UP NO MORE.
WE'LL FIND ANOTHER GANG, AND WHEN WE DO, WE'LL DO BETTER. WE'LL BE SMART. FROM NOW ON, IT'S A NEW ROCKSTEADY AND BEBOP...
...ME AND A GROUP OF GUYS WORK FOR A GUY WHO WORKS FOR ANOTHER GUY—
—WHO WORKS FOR THE FOOT CLAN. EVER HEAR OF IT? COURSE YOU HAVEN'T, CUZ WE'RE THE BEST, MAN. TOTALLY STEALTH,

—VOLUNTEERS FOR THIS "SPECIAL UNIT" WILL BE TAKING A QUANTUM LEAP IN STATUS. IF YOU ARE CONTENT AT THE BOTTOM OF THE FOOT CLAN, CONTENT WITH BEING INFERIOR, THEN CONTINUE TO WASTE YOUR LIFE. BUT IF YOU WANT MORE FOR YOURSELF...
...THEN JOIN ME. THOSE WHO PROVE THEMSELVES WORTHY WILL ONE DAY BECOME THE ULTIMATE FOOT SOLDIERS...
...I OFFER YOU A CHANCE TO BECOME *MUTANTS!*
WE WANNA GO BIGGER. WE WANT THE NEXT FIGHT TO BE FREAK AGAINST FREAK.
YEAH, WHEN DO WE GET TO CHANGE ALREADY?
"I NEED ONLY TWO OF YOU.
"AND SO, WE WILL CONDUCT ONE FINAL TEST TO DETERMINE WHO WILL MOVE FORWARD.
"LAST ONES STANDING STAY."
WE DID IT, ROCKSTEADY. YOU KNOW WHAT THIS MEANS?
I WANNA BE A DINOSAUR! WONDER IF THEY GOT THAT.
HEH HEH, OH YEAH. NICE CHOMPERS.
RHINO-SAURUS! NICE!
REINDEER
RHINOCEROS

BEBO

YOUR TWO WEEKS OF TRAINING ARE COMPLETE. YOU ARE READY.

READY TO MEE SHREDDE
NOT YET. TONIGHT YOU WILL COME WITH ME ON A JOB FOR A LITTLE FIELD TEST. IT'S TIME WE TRY YOU IN AN UNCONTROLLED ENVIRONMENT.

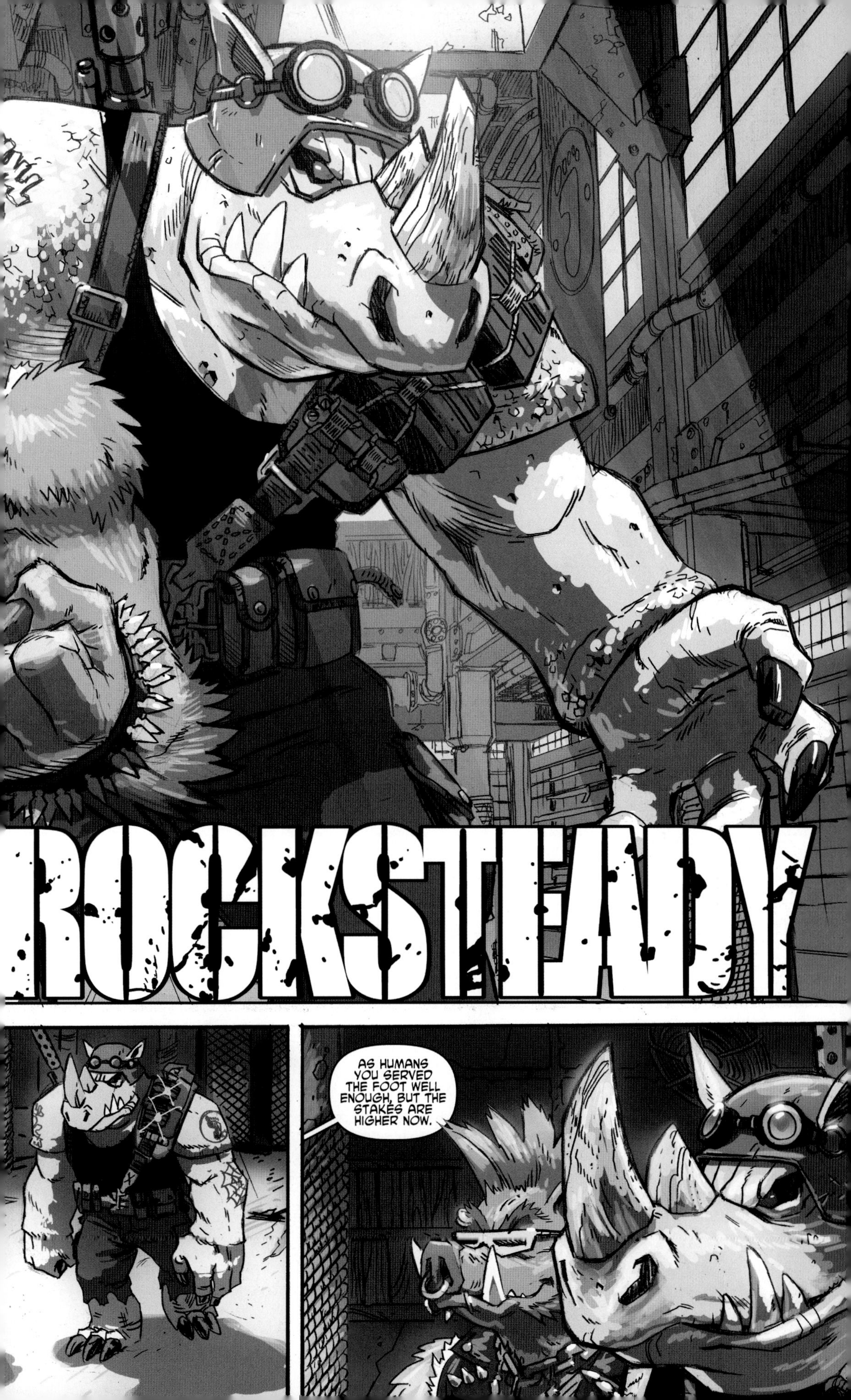

ROCKSTEADY

AS HUMANS YOU SERVED THE FOOT WELL ENOUGH, BUT THE STAKES ARE HIGHER NOW.

CAN YOU BELIEVE THIS? WE MADE IT, MAN!
YEAH, WE'RE IN THE BEST GANG EVER—THE FOOT CLAN.
AND WE'RE SUPER KICK-ASS MUTANTS!
JUST LOOK AT ME. ARE YOU GOING TO MESS WITH A GUY WHO LOOKS LIKE THIS? I DON'T THINK SO.
HAHAHA! YEAH! I'VE GOT A HORN ON MY NOSE. HOW GREAT IS THAT?

AND, ROCKSTEADY, WE WORK FOR THE SHREDDER NOW. HE'S TAKING OVER ALL OF NEW YORK.
HE'S LIKE THE KING OF NEW YORK.
THAT MAKES US LIKE THE DUKES OF NEW YORK.
OH YEAH! I BET THE SHREDDER IS LIKE THE COOLEST!
HEY, DO YOU THINK THE SHREDDER WOULD DIG IT IF I WORE TURTLE SHELLS FOR SHOULDER PADS?
HAHA, HE DOES HAVE A PROBLEM WITH TURTLES...

I BET THE GUY WOULD LOVE IT.
DUDE, HE'S GOING TO LOVE US! WE'RE GOING TO BE BEST FRIENDS!
HA HA HA HA

SLAP

THE MASTER IS NO ONE'S FRIEND!

"AH KARAI. I SEE YOU BROUGHT SOME *WILDLIFE*."
I HAD HEARD OF THE FOX WOMAN, BUT THIS...
...THE FOOT CLAN IS FULL OF SURPRISES.
XIANG FEI TONG
YOUR LETTER DIDN'T SAY WHY YOU'RE COMING, BUT I BELIEVE I KNOW WHAT BRINGS YOU HERE. PLEASE, JOIN ME FOR TEA IN MY PRIVATE OFFICE.
THIS IS A PRETTY SWEET GIG, HUH, GUYS?

YOU JUST BROKE HIS NOSE! YOU ARE GOING TO PAY FOR THAT, *FREAK!*
HEY FELLAS, DON'T GO STARTING TROUBLE, OKAY?

I KNOW HOW THIS MUST BE FOR YOU, XIANG. I SEE WHAT YOU'VE BUILT HERE. I SEE THAT YOU ARE *PROUD* OF THIS GANG...

...BUT PRIDE CLOUDS YOUR JUDGMENT. THE FOOT CLAN IS A FORCE THAT YOUR GANG CAN'T CONTEND WITH. IF YOU DISRESPECT THE RULE OF THE SHREDDER AND FAIL TO ATTEND THIS UPCOMING CEREMONY, YOU AND YOUR GHOST BOYS WILL BE ERASED FROM THIS CITY.

WHY, KARAI, OF COURSE WE WILL BE ATTENDING.
YOUR VISIT HERE, THREATENING ME, IT WAS FOR NOTHING. I AM LOOKING FORWARD TO THE CEREMONY.
BOOM!
CRASH
RATATATATATATATA
KA-BOOM
WHAT IS THIS?!
WHAT HAVE YOU DONE?!
UH... THINGS GOT A LITTLE INTENSE OUT HERE. WE'VE GOT IT UNDER CONTROL THOUGH.

SO YOU'VE BROUGHT YOUR MONSTERS HERE TO DESTROY US IN OUR OWN HOME. CHEN, KILL HER NOW!
Ch-Chak
OH NO YOU DON'T!
THIS IS COWARDLY AND UNDERHANDED, EVEN FOR THE FOOT! AND THE SHREDDER EXPECTS ME TO SUBMIT TO HIM? NEVER!
IT'S OKAY. I'M ALL RIGHT.
DON'T WORRY, BOSS. I GOT HER!
YEAH, LEAVE THIS TO US, BOSS.
THIS ENDS NOW...

IT'S LIKE SHE'S INHUMANLY FAST. I KNOW WE'RE THE MUTANTS BUT SHE'S FREAKISHLY FAST, AM I RIGHT?
I GOT AN IDEA!
WE'LL CUT HER OFF AT THE PASS!
BOOM
ROCKSTEADY, YOU'RE A GENIUS!

YOU MISSED HER! SHE'S RIGHT HERE, YOU BOZO!
THE GHOST BOYS WILL NEVER BOW TO TRASH!
FIRST YOU RUIN THIS MEETING, NOW YOU INSULT *THE MIGHT OF THE FOOT CLAN?*

BOOM
WHAT ARE YOU DOING? YOUR HORN ALMOST POKED MY EYE OUT, YOU JERK!
WHO YOU CALLING A JERK, YOU GUMBALL? I WOULDA HAD HER IF YOU WASN'T IN MY WAY!
BLAM-BLAM
HEY, THAT TICKLES, YOU LITTLE CREEPS!

STOP!
POLICE!

CRASH

EAT THIS, SUCKERS!

OH, MAN. WE SCREWED UP, BEBOP.
KARAI WAS IN THERE.

I THINK WE JUST KILLED KARAI!
...

...THE GHOST GUYS STARTED IT. NONE OF THIS WOULD HAVE HAPPENED IF THEY HADN'T STARTED IT.
AND ALSO, THESE CHINATOWN BUILDINGS, THEY'RE JUST NOT MADE GOOD. I THINK THEY'RE *MADE* IN CHINA.
BEBOP, KARAI IS DEAD. AND WE PROBABLY ALSO KILLED WHATEVER DEAL THEY WERE TRYING TO MAKE WITH THE GHOST GUYS. WE SCREWED UP! WE SCREWED UP *AGAIN!*

YOU'RE RIGHT. SHREDDER'S GONNA KICK US OUT OF THE GANG FOR SURE!... OR WORSE!
WHAT COULD BE WORSE THAN GETTING KICKED OUT?

HE'LL KILL US.
EASY. WE'LL POUND HIM INTO LETTING US WORK FOR HIM!
AWAY, OR JOINED THE GHOST BOYS.
SHE DECIDED THAT THE GHOST BOYS WERE A BETTER FIT FOR HER OR SOMETHING.
FOOSS
Thwip Thwip
Thwip
HUH?
WHAM
YOU GUYS GOT IT ALL WRONG.
WE WAS JUST DOIN' OUR JOB. THE GHOST BOYS STARTED THE FIGHT, AND THEN KARAI RAN AWAY.
YEAH, SHE SAID NOBODY UNDERSTANDS ME, AND SO ON.

YOU TWO HAVE DISHONORED THE FOOT CLAN AND BROUGHT ME SHAME. I KNEW THAT YOU WERE STUPID BUT THIS... IT'S TIME TO CUT MY LOSSES.

GOODBYE, BEBOP AND ROCKSTEADY.

YOU CAN'T KICK US OUT.

I KNOW WE MESSED UP... BUT WE CAN DO BETTER.
WE AIN'T GOING BACK TO BEING LOSERS. JUST DON'T KICK US OUT.
EVEN WHEN THE FOOT CLAN ATTEMPTS TO KILL YOU... YOU STILL WISH TO BELONG?

WELL, SURE. THE FOOT CLAN IS THE BEST THERE IS.
PLUS, NO ONE ELSE WILL HAVE US. WE'VE BEEN KICKED OUT OF EVERY OTHER GANG.

VIOLENCE. DES
I SEE NOW THA
ALL YOU ARE G
TODAY, I'M LE
LIVE. BUT NEVE
YOUR LIVES NO
TO THE F
DEFEATING FOOT SOLDIERS IS ONE THING, BUT TO ME YOU ARE VULNERABLE IDIOTS WHOM I HAVE NO PROBLEM KILLING.

SORRY WE RUINED THINGS WITH THE GHOST GUYS.

XIANG FEI TONG WAS AN ARROGANT FOOL. SHE PLANNED TO MAKE AN ATTEMPT ON SHREDDER'S LIFE... THE GHOST BOYS' DEMISE WAS INEVITABLE.

I THINK THAT MEANS WE'RE STILL IN!
YEAH... I HOPE SHREDDER AIN'T AS MEAN AS HER.
OF COURSE HE AIN'T. YOU THINK YOU CAN BECOME THE KING OF ALL OF NEW YORK BY BEING A JERK?

LATER THAT NIGHT.
THEEEEEEEY'RE ROCKSTEADY AND BEBOP—
—THEY'RE STRONG TO THE FINISH—
AND THEY JUST DON'T STOP—!
THEY'LL BEAT YOU WITH FISTS, WITH A BAT, WITH A KNIFE—
SO DON'T TRY TO STOP THEM—JUST RUN FOR YOUR LIFE—
GET SET AND GET READY—FOR BEBOOOOOP AND-ROCKSTEADYYYYY!
HAHA HAHA!

Art by Ben Bates

Art by Mike Henderson

Art by **Marley Zarcone**

Art by **Mike Henderson**

Art by Chris Uminga

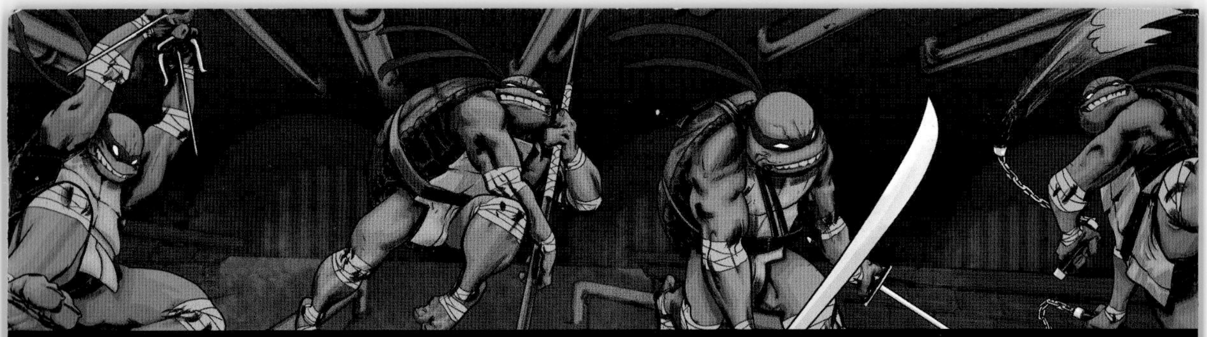

TEENAGE MUTANT NINJA TURTLES

MORE TURTLE ACTION!

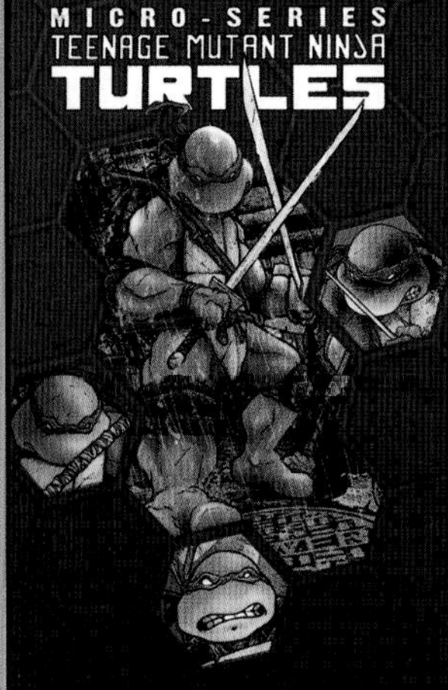

TEENAGE MUTANT NINJA TURTLES: MICRO-SERIES, VOL. 1
ISBN: 978-1-61377-232-4

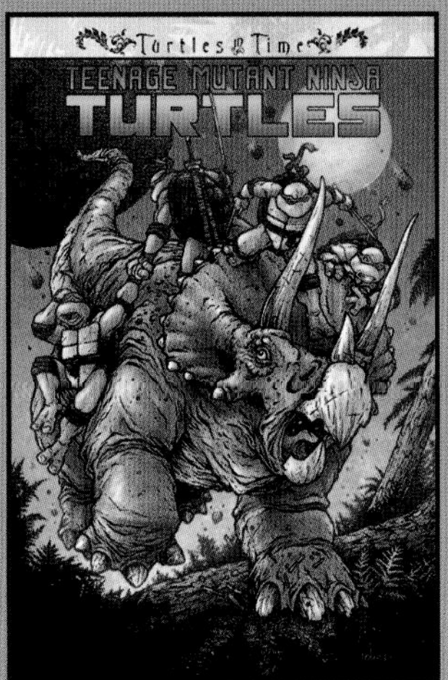

TEENAGE MUTANT NINJA TURTLES: TURTLES IN TIME
ISBN: 978-1-63140-181-7

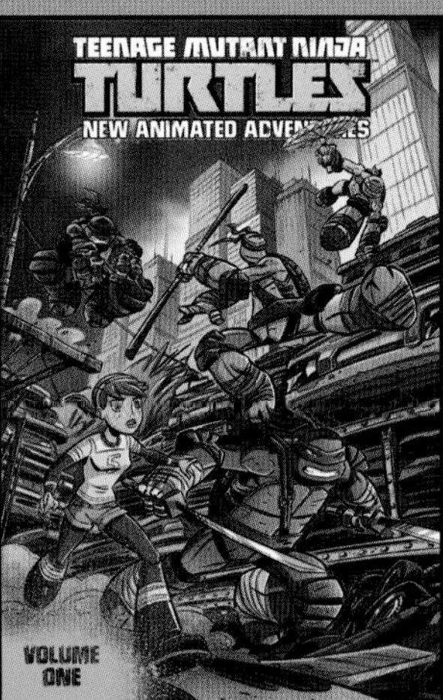

TEENAGE MUTANT NINJA TURTLES: NEW ANIMATED ADVENTURES, VOL. 1
ISBN: 978-1-61377-856-2

TEENAGE MUTANT NINJA TURTLES: THE ULTIMATE COLLECTION, VOL. 1
ISBN: 978-1-61377-007-8

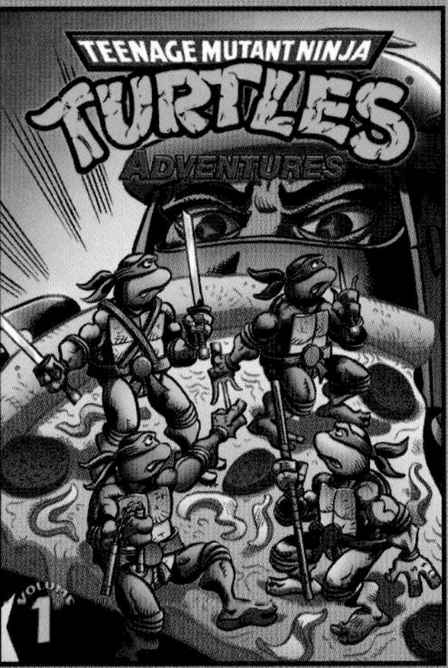

TEENAGE MUTANT NINJA TURTLES ADVENTURES, VOL. 1
ISBN: 978-1-61377-289-8

TEENAGE MUTANT NINJA TURTLES, VOL. 1: CHANGE IS CONSTANT
ISBN: 978-1-61377-139-6

ON SALE NOW

nickelodeon

IDW
www.idwpublishing.com